An Introduction to the Grammar of English

An Introduction
to the Grammar of English

Syntactic arguments and
socio-historical background

Elly van Gelderen
Arizona State University

John Benjamins Publishing Company
Amsterdam / Philadelphia

™ The paper used in this publication meets the minimum requirements of American National Standard for Information Sciences – Permanence of Paper for Printed Library Materials, ANSI z39.48-1984.

Library of Congress Cataloging-in-Publication Data

Gelderen, Elly van.
    An introduction to the grammar of English : syntactic arguments and socio-historical background / Elly van Gelderen.
      p. cm.
    Includes bibliographical references and index.
    1. English language--Grammar. 2. English language--Grammar, Historical. 3. English language--Social aspects. 4. English language--Syntax. I. Title.

PE1106.G38 2002
428.2-dc21   2002021580

ISBN 90 272 2588 5 (Eur.) / ISBN 1 58811 200 4 (US) (Hb; alk. paper)
ISBN 90 272 2586 9 (Eur.) / ISBN 1 58811 157 1 (US) (Pb; alk. paper)

John Benjamins Publishing Co. · P.O. Box 36224 · 1020 ME Amsterdam · The Netherlands
John Benjamins North America · P.O. Box 27519 · Philadelphia PA 19118-0519 · USA

Table of contents

Preface

To the student

You don't have to read long novels in this course — no *Middlemarch* or *War and Peace*. There isn't much memorization either. It should be enough if you become familiar with the keywords at the end of each chapter (use the glossary, but don't overemphasize the importance of terminology). The focus is on arguments, exercises, and tree drawing. You need to do this from the first week on, however, and you may also have to read a chapter more than once. The course is not particularly difficult but once you get lost, go for help! The book is divided in four parts, with review sections after each. Chapter 1 is the introduction; skip the 'justification' if you want.

Justification and thanks

This grammar is in the tradition of the Quirk family of grammars, such as the work of Huddleston, Burton-Roberts, Aarts & Wekker. Quirk, Greenbaum, Leech, and Svartvik's work in turn is based on a long tradition of grammarians such as Jespersen, Kruisinga, Poutsma, and Zandvoort.

While following the traditional distinction between function (subject, object, etc.) and realization (NP, VP, etc), the present book focusses on the structure and makes the function derivative, as in more generativist work, making it unlike recent grammars such as Verspoor & Sauter (2000). Its focus on structure can be seen in the treatment of the VP as consisting of the verb and its complements. Abstract discussions such as what a constituent is are largely avoided (in fact, the term constituent is since it is a stumbling block in my experience), and the structure of the NP and AP is brought in line with that of the VP: NPs and APs have complements as well as modifiers.

A clear distinction is made between lexical and functional (here called grammatical) categories. Lexical categories project to phrases and these phrases have functions at sentence level (subject, predicate, object). As in traditional grammar, but unlike in generative grammar, functional categories (determiner, auxiliary, coordinator, and complementizer) do not project to phrases and have no function at sentence level (they function exclusively inside a phrase and connect clauses and phrases). Hence, determiner, auxiliary, coordinator and complementizer express realization as well as function. This distinction is of course not always clearcut, e.g. adverbs, pronouns, and some prepositions are in between. I do bring this up.

On occasion, I do not give a definitive solution to a problem because there isn't any. This lack of explanation can be caused either by an analysis remaining controversial, as in the case of ditransitive verbs and coordinates, or by the continual changes taking place in English (or any other language for that matter). Instead of giving one solution, I discuss some options. I have found that students become frustrated if, for instance, they can reasonably argue that a verb is prepositional in contexts where 'the book says' it is an intransitive verb. Therefore, the emphasis in this book is on the argumentation, and not on presenting 'the' solution. The chapter where I have been quite conservative in my analysis is Chapter 6. The reason is that to provide the argumentation for a non-flat structure involves theta-theory and quantifier-float and this leads too far afield.

Unlike Quirk et al. (1985), this grammar starts with a chapter on intuitive linguistic knowledge and provides an explanation for it based on Universal Grammar. Also different is the discussion of prescriptive rules, at the end of each chapter. In my experience, students want to know what the prescriptive rule is. Strangely enough, they don't want the instructor to tell them that linguistically speaking, there is nothing wrong with splitting an infinitive or using *like* as a complementizer. Adding those topics is a compromise to them. I have not integrated them in the chapters since I want to keep descriptive and prescriptive rules separate. The topics, obviously, cannot cover all traditional usage questions, such as the 'correct' past participle or subjunctive forms. They are added to give a flavor for the kinds of prescriptive rules around.

The chapters in this book cover 'standard' material: categories, phrases, functions, and embedded sentences. There are a few sections that I have labelled optional, since, depending on the course, they may be too complex. The last chapter could either be skipped or expanded upon, depending on whether it is appropriate to introduce S″ or CP. It should be possible to cover all chapters in one semester. The students I have in mind (because of my own teaching background) are English, Humanities, Philosophy, and Education majors as well as others taking an upper level grammar course in an English department at a North American university, or those in an English department in a European country. Textbooks for such courses have 'grammar' in their titles rather than 'syntax', and hence the title of this book. I am assuming students using this book know basic 'grammar', for instance, the past tense of *go*, and the comparative of *good*. Students who do not have that knowledge should consult a work such as O'Dwyer (2000).

Even though I know there is a danger in giving *one* answer where more than one are sometimes possible, I have nevertheless provided answers to the exercises. It is done to avoid having to go over all exercises in class. I hope this makes it possible to concentrate on those exercises that are interesting or challenging.

I would like to thank my students in earlier grammar courses whose frustration with some of the inconsistencies in other books has inspired the current work. I am sure this is not the first work so begun. I am extremely grateful to Johanna Wood for long, helpful discussions which made me rethink how to present fundamental questions and for suggesting the special topics. Johanna also made extensive comments to the exercises. I also thank Harry Bracken for his comments and encouragement, Viktorija Todorovska for major editorial comments, Tom Stroik for supportive suggestions, Barbara Fennell for detailed comments and insightful clarifications, and Anke de Looper of John Benjamins for creative solutions regarding the published version. Other suggestions on the e-text as well on the paper version and on the general project by Dhira Mahoney, Lutfi Hussein, Jeff Parker, Laura Parsons, Mariana Bahtchevanova and Susan Miller were much appreciated.

List of tables

Glossary

At the end of each chapter, there is a list of key terms. These are the most relevant and should be understood.

The glossary tries to be somewhat comprehensive, and lists key terms, abbreviations, non-key terms, and some common terminology not used in this book, e.g. attributive adjective, but perhaps used elsewhere. Don't attempt to memorize the glossary!

Adj′	Adjective-bar, intermediate category, see Chapter 9, Section 1.
accusative case	The case of the object or prepositional object, only visible on pronouns in English, e.g. *me*, in *He saw me*, also called the objective case. See special topic to Chapter 4.
active	A sentence in which the doer of the action is the subject, as in *I saw an elephant*, see Chapter 4, Section 1.3.
Adj	= adjective, see below.
adjective	A word which often describes qualities, e.g. *proud*; it modifies a noun, see Chapter 2, Section 1.2.
adjective complement	Complement to an adjective, e.g. *of him* in *proud [of him]*, see Chapter 9, Section 1.
AdjP	= Adjective Phrase: group of words centered around an adjective, e.g. *very nice*, see Chapter 3, Section 1.3.
adjunct	Term not used in this book; alternative for 'adverbial', see there.
Adv	= adverb, see below.
adverb	E.g. *proudly*; it is similar to an adjective but it modifies a verb, adjective, or other adverb, see Chapter 2, Section 1.2, whereas an adjective modifies a noun.
adverbial	A function at sentence level providing the background on where, when, how, and why the event described in the VP takes place, see Chapter 5, Section 1.
AdvP	= Adverb Phrase: group of words centered around an adverb, e.g. *very nicely*, see Chapter 3, Section 1.3.
affix	Cannot stand on its own, e.g. an ending such as *-ing*, see Chapter 2, Section 1.1, Chapter 6, and Table 6.3.

affix-hop	Process where an affix belonging to an auxiliary 'hops' and attaches to the verb immediately to the right of the auxiliary, see Chapter 6 and Table 6.3.
agreement	E.g. -s in *she walks*, ending on the verb that 'agrees' with the subject, see special topic Chapter 9.
ambiguity/ambiguous	Word (lexical ambiguity) or sentence (structural ambiguity) with more than one meaning, see Chapters 1 and 3.
antecedent	What a pronoun refers to, e.g. the noun that a relative pronoun such as *who* refers to in *the man who(m) I saw*, see Chapter 10. Antecedent is used more generally though for any pronoun that refers to a noun.
antonym	A word with the opposite meaning, e.g. *hot/cold, good/bad*, Chapter 2.
appositive NP	The second NP in *Tegucigalpa, the capital of Honduras*, see Chapter 3. It rephrases the first and provides extra information; similar to a non-restrictive relative clause.
appositive relative clause	Another word for non-restrictive relative clasue, see Chapter 10 and below.
article	*A, an, the* in English, see Chapter 2, Section 2.1.
aspect	When the character of the action is emphasized, as in *he is reading*, rather than when the action took place, Chapter 6, Section 1.3.
attributive adjective	Term not used in this book; an adjective that modifies a Noun inside an NP.
AUX	= auxiliary, see below.
auxiliary	A 'verb' that cannot stand on its own, but that 'helps' (combines with) another verb, e.g. *have* in *They have seen a riot*, see Chapters 2 and 6 and Table 6.1.
bare infinitive	Infinitive without a *to*, e.g. *leave* in *I saw her leave*, see Chapter 8.
branch	A line that marks the relationship between two nodes in tree; it shows how a phrase is divided up, see Chapter 3, Section 1.
BrE	British English
C	= complementizer, see below.
case	In English, case is only visible on pronouns. Thus, *she* in *She saw me* has nominative case, i.e. is used in subject position, and *me* has accusative or objective case, i.e. is used in object position.
clause	Unit containing a lexical verb, see also main clause, subordinate clause, see Chapters 7, 8, and 10.
cleft	A construction of the form *It is Catweazle who caused the problems*, see Chapter 11, Section 3.
coathanger	Not dividing a phrase into separate branches (to save space); used rarely in this book, see Chapters 3 and 11.
comma splice	A comma between two independent clauses, see extra topic Chapter 11.
comparative	Forms such as *greater* that compare one situation or entity with another.

complement	Complement to V, N, Adj, P. Complements to Vs are divided into direct and indirect object, subject predicate, object predicate, prepositional and phrasal object. Nouns, adjectives, and prepositions can also have complements, see Chapters 3, 9, and 10.
complementizer	E.g. *that/if/whether*, connects two clauses, one subordinate to the other, see Chapters 2 and 7.
complex transitive	A verb with a direct object and an object predicate, see Chapter 4, Section 2.
conjunction	Not used in this book, except in quotes and to indicate an alternative phrasing. It is a general term to describe a word that joins two or more words or phrases or sentences together. There are subordinating (*that*) and coordinating (*and*) conjunctions, see Chapter 2, Section 2.3.
consonant	Sound such as *b, p, f, v, t, k*, made by somehow modifying the airstream, see Chapter 1, 1.1. for use in a rule.
constituent	Not used in this book; a group of words that form a unit, typically a phrase.
contraction	Two words that become one, e.g. *he's* for *he has*, see special topic Chapter 6.
coordination	The process of connecting two phrases or clauses that are equal to each other by means of e.g. *and*, see Chapter 3, Section 3.
coordinating conjunction	Not used in this book; same as coordinator, see there.
coordinator	Connects two phrases or clauses that are equal to each other, e.g. *and/or*, see Chapter 2, also called coordinating conjunction.
copula	A verb with a subject predicative, typically *to be* or *to become*, see Chapter 4, Section 2.
CP	Complementizer Phrase. Similar to S', but in a framework where grammatical categories project. Not used in this book.
D	= determiner, see below.
(D)Adv	Degree adverb, see below, and usually designated as Adv.
dangling modifier	An adverbial clause whose subject is not the same as the subject of the main sentence, see special topic Chapter 8.
daughter	For example, P is a daughter of a PP, i.e. lower in the tree but connected to the 'mother' by a branch, see Chapter 3, Section 2, Table 2.3.
degree adverb	Adverbs that indicate degree, e.g. *very, too, so, more, most, quite, rather*, see Chapter 2, Section 1.2.
descriptivism	Describing what language users really say, as opposed to what they 'should' say, see Chapter 1.
determiner	Word that points or specifies, e.g. *the*, see Chapter 2, Section 2.1.
direct object	Object of a verb such as *eat, see*, and *enjoy*. For instance, *him* in *They saw him*, see Chapter 4, Section 1.2.
ditransitive	Verb that has both a direct and indirect object, e.g. *tell, give*, see Chapter 4, Section 2.

DO	=direct object, see above.
DP	Determiner Phrase. A phrase with the determiner as head and the NP as sister to D. Not used in this book.
dummy	A word used to fulfill a grammatical requirement, see dummy *do* and dummy subject below.
dummy *do*	If no auxiliary is present in a sentence, *do* is used with questions and negatives, see Chapter 6, 1.5.
dummy subject	If a subject is not present, *it* or *there* are used, also see pleonastic subject, Chapter 4, Section 1.1, and Chapter 7.
echo question	Question formed by special intonation, as in *You saw WHAT?* See Chapter 11, Section 1.2.
ed-participle	See past participle.
e.g.	Short for 'for example' from Latin *exempli gratia*.
elided/elision	Letter or syllable deleted or left out for ease of pronunciation. Terms not used in this book.
ellipsis	Words deleted or left out to avoid repetition, e.g. in *He wrote a poem and painted some pictures*, there is ellipsis of the subject of *painted*.
embedded sentence/clause	A clause or sentence inside another phrase or sentence/clause, see Chapter 7.
emphasizer	Words such as *even* and *just* that are used to emphasize a phrase, also called focusser, see Chapter 9.
exclamation	Sentences such as *Man, what a fool he is!!*, see Chapter 11, Section 2.
extraposed/ extraposition	When an embedded clause (usually in subject position) is placed at the end of the sentence, e.g. *It was nice [that he left]*. A dummy subject *it* is put in the original position. See Chapter 7, Section 3.
finite clause	A clause with a finite verb (see below) and a nominative subject, see Chapter 7.
finite verb	A verb expressing agreement and tense (past or present), see Chapters 6 and 7.
flat structure	A tree that does not express hierarchies because many branches descend from one node, see Chapter 3, Section 1.1.
focusser	Words such as *even* and *just* that are used to emphasize a phrase, also called emphasizer, see Chapter 9.
formal language	Language used in formal situations such as ceremonies, formal lectures, meeting a government official, see Chapter 1.
functional category	Not used in this book, alternative to grammatical category.
functions	Phrases (and clauses) have functions such as Subject and Direct Object. These are at the level of the sentence. There are also functions inside the phrase, namely determiner, modifier, and complement. See Chapters 4 and 5 for functions at sentence level and Chapters 9 and 10 for functions at phrase level.

gender	In English, the distinction between masculine pronouns such as *he, his,* and *himself* and feminine ones such as *she, her,* and *herself.*
genitive case	The case that a possessive has, e.g. *Catweazle's* in *Catweazle's book,* see special topics Chapter 4.
gerund	A verbal noun that ends in *-ing.* When it has a subject, this subject bears genitive case e.g. *John's* in *John's cleaning up would be appreciated,* briefly discussed in Chapter 8, Section 1, and Chapter 10, Section 1.
gradable	Not used in this book. Adjective that can be modified in terms of degree, e.g. *very happy, happier.*
grammar	The rules to form and understand language. In this book, we focus on how to analyze sentences, rather than full texts, words, or sounds. We also focus on descriptive, rather than prescriptive rules.
grammatical	A sentence (or word) that native speakers consider acceptable.
grammatical category	Word with little meaning, e.g. Determiner, Quantifier, Auxiliary, Coordinator and Complementizer, see Chapter 2.
head	The most important part of a unit/phrase, e.g. the N *seadog* is the head of the NP *the blue seadog,* see Chapter 9.
hypercorrection	When speakers are so conscious that a prescriptive rule exists that they make a mistake.
i.e.	Short for 'namely', from Latin *id est.*
ing-participle	See present participle.
imperative	A command such as *Go away, shut up!,* see Chapter 6, Section 3.
indicative	A 'normal' sentence, i.e. not asking a question, indicating a wish or command, mentioned in Chapter 11, but not emphasized.
indirect object	Object that can be preceded by *to* or *for,* e.g. *Doris* in *Clovis gave Doris a flower,* see Chapter 4, Section 1.2.
infinitive	Form such as *to go, to be, to analyze;* it is one of the non-finite constructions. See Chapter 8.
informal language	Language used in informal situations such as casual conversation. In/formality depends on the situation, the participants, the topic. See Chapter 1.
innate faculty	Enables us to acquire language, see Chapter 1.
interrogative pronoun	Pronouns that indicate a *wh*-question such as *who left,* see Chapter 11. They are in form similar to relative pronouns.
interrogative sentence	A question such as *who will go there,* see Chapter 11.
intransitive	A verb without an object, e.g. *laugh, swim,* see Chapter 4, Section 2.
IO	=indirect object, see above.
IP	Inflection Phrase. A phrase where tense and agreement (Inflection) are seen as the head. Similair to S but not used in this book.
irregular verbs	The past tense and past participle of these verbs are not formed by adding *-ed* to the present, as in the case of regular verbs. Some examples of irregular verbs are: *go, went, gone; see, saw, seen; write, wrote, written.* See special topic Chapter 6.

lexical category	Word with lexical meaning, such as a Noun, Verb, Adjective, Adverb, and Preposition, see Chapter 2, Section 1.
lexical verb	Verb that can stand on its own, e.g. *see, walk*, see Chapter 2, Section 1.1, and Chapter 6.
light verb	Verbs such as *make, do, take* with a very general meaning that combine with nouns, such as *take a walk*. They can be replaced by verbs, e.g. *walk*, Chapter 4.
linguistic knowledge	Knowledge about linguistic notions and rules that we have in our heads, e.g. consonants and vowels, structure, question formation, see Chapter 1.
linguistics	The study of language.
main clause	Independent clause, i.e. a sentence that can stand on its own, minimally containing a subject and a predicate and not embedded within another clause.
modal	Auxiliary such as *must, will, would, can, could* that expresses necessity, uncertainty, possibility, see Chapter 6.
modifier	An element whose function is to modify another element, e.g. *purple* in *purple sage*, see Chapter 9.
modify	Describe the quality of something.
monotransitive	See transitive.
morphology	Rules for how to build words, e.g. *formal + ize*, see Chapter 1.
mother	In a tree, the node above another node, e.g. PP is the mother of P.
multiple negation	When two or more negative words (*not, nobody*) occur in the same clause to indicate negation, e.g. *I didn't eat nothing*, see special topic Chapter 3.
N	= noun, see below.
N′	= N-bar, intermediate category, see Chapters 3 and 9.
negation/negative	E.g. the adverbs *not* or *n't*, see Chapters 2 and 6, or a negative word such as *nothing*.
node	A point in the tree, e.g. NP is a node, see Chapter 3.
nominative case	The case of the subject, only visible on pronouns, e.g. *she* in *She left early*, see special topic Chapter 4.
non-finite verb or clause	A verb that lacks tense and a nominative subject, e.g. *to be or not to be*, see Chapter 6, Section 3, and Chapter 8.
non-linguistic (or social) knowledge	Knowledge of social rules, see Chapter 1, Section 3.
non-restrictive RC	A clause that provides background information to the noun it modifies; is often set apart from the rest of the sentence through commas or comma intonation, see Chapter 10, Section 2, also called appositive clause.
noun	A word such as *table, freedom, book, love*, see Chapter 2; Table 2.1.
noun complement	*Of chemistry* in *teacher of chemistry*, see Chapter 10, Section 2.

NP	= Noun Phrase, group of words centered around a noun, e.g. *the red balloon*, see Chapter 3, Section 1.1.
number	Singular and plural number appears in English on pronouns and as verbal agreement.
numeral	A word such as *one, two*. They can be seen as Adj or D, see Chapter 2 and Table 2.3.
NYT	Abbreviation for the *New York Times*.
objective or accusative case	In English, case is only visible on pronouns, e.g *him*, in *Hermione saw him*. Objects typically get this case, hence the name objective. See special topics, Chapter 4.
object predicate	Often realized as an AdjP, NP, or PP, making a claim about the object, e.g. *nice* in *I consider her nice*. It occurs together with a complex transitive verb such as *consider, elect*, see Chapter 4, Section 1.3.
OED	Oxford English Dictionary, see references.
P	= preposition, see below.
participle	Either accompanied by an auxiliary, see Chapter 6, or on its own heading a non-finite clause, see Chapter 8, Section 2.
particle	Similar in form to prepositions and adverbs, but only used together with a verb, see Chapter 2, Section 1.3, and Chapter 5, Sections 3 and 4, also discussion K.
passive auxiliary	A form of *to be* used together with a past participle. For instance, *was* in *She was arrested*, see Chapter 6, Section 1.4.
passive construction	A construction where what looks like an object is functioning as a subject, e.g. *she* in *She was arrested*, see Chapter 4, Section 1.3, and Chapter 6, Section 1.4.
past participle	Typically follows auxiliary *to have* to form a perfect, or *to be* to form a passive. It can function on it own in a non-finite clause. The participle ends in *-ed/-en (walked, written, chosen)* or may be irregular, such as *gone, swum, begun, learnt*.
perfect auxiliary	*To have* when used together with a past participle. For instance, *have* in *I have done that already*.
person	The distinction between, for instance, first person *I*, second person *you*, and third person *they* is one of person.
personal pronoun	A pronoun that can function on its own, e.g. as a subject or object, see Chapter 3, Section 3.
phonology	The structure of the sound system, see Chapter 1.
phrasal verb	A verb that is always combined with a preposition-like element but which has a special meaning. For instance, *look up* does not mean 'see upwards', but 'go to the library and check on something', see Chapter 5, Section 3.
phrase	A group of related word, centered around a head, see Chapter 3.
pied piping	Taking the preposition along in a relative clause or a question, as in *the man to whom I talked*, see Chapter 10.

pleonastic subject	see dummy subject, see also Chapter 4, Section 1.1.
possessive pronoun	E.g. *his* or *Catweazle's* in *his book* or *Catweazle's book*, see Chapter 2, Section 2.1.
postmodifier	Modifier that follows the head, e.g. *from Venus* in *a stone from Venus*, see Chapter 9.
PP	= Preposition Phrase: group of words belonging to the preposition, e.g. *in the garden*, see Chapter 3, Section 1.4.
pre-D	= Pre-determiner, quantifiers such as *all, both, half* can occur before the determiner, e.g. in *all that trouble*, see Chapter 2, Section 2.2.
predicate	Says something about the subject, typically a VP, e.g. *saw him* in *Hermione saw him*, see Chapter 4, Section 1.1.
predicative adjective	Term not used in this book; an adjective that heads an AP with the function of subject predicate or object predicate.
premodifier	Modifier that precedes the head, e.g. *blue* in *a blue hat*, see Chapter 9.
preposing	Moving a word or phrase to a position towards the beginning of a sentence.
preposition	A word indicating location (in place and time), such as *at, in, on*, direction, such as *to, into, towards*, relationship, such as *with, between, among, of*, see Chapter 2, Section 1.3.
preposition stranding	Leaving the preposition behind in a relative clause or a question, as in *the man who I talked to*, see Chapter 10.
prepositional verb	A verb that has a PP as a complement, e.g. *rely on, refer to*, see Chapter 5, Section 2.
prescriptivism	A rule typically learned in school, see Chapter 1, e.g. don't split an infinitive or don't use multiple negation.
present participle	Forms that end in *-ing*, e.g. *walking*, used after a progressive auxiliary, as in *he is walking*, or on its own in a non-finite clause, as in *Walking along the street, I saw a fire*.
progressive	Indicating that the action is or was going on, see Chapter 6, Section 1.3.
projection	The expansion of a head upwards in the tree. For instance, a V projects to a VP.
pronominalization	Referring to an NP, PP, VP, AdjP, or AdvP by means of a pronoun, e.g. Chapter 3, Section 1.
pronoun	Words such as *he, she, it, me* that refer to an NP; pronouns replacing PPs (*there*), AdjPs (*so*), AdvPs (*thus*), or VPs (*do so*) are called either pronoun or pro-form, see Chapter 3, Section 3.
pseudo-cleft	A construction such as *What he did was stupid*, used to emphasize/focus a part, see Chapter 11, Section 3.
pun	The use of a word to suggest two meanings, see Chapter 1.
quantifier	Words such as *all, some, many, each*; they are either like determiners or adjectives, or occur before determiners, see Chapter 2 and Table 2.3.
question	See *Yes/No* Question and *wh*-Question, and Chapter 11, Section 1.
RC	= relative clause, see below and Chapter 10, Sections 2 and 3.

regular verbs	Verbs formed by adding -*ed* to the present to form the past tense and the past participle, as in the case of regular verbs such as *walk, walked, walked.*
relative clause	A clause/sentence that typically modifies a noun, e.g. *the tree which I see from the window,* see Chapter 10, Section 2.
relative pronoun	pronoun such as *who, whose* that introduces relative clauses, Chapter 10. The same set is used in questions and then they are called interrogative pronouns.
restrictive RC	A relative clause with highly relevant information, see Table 10.1.
S	= sentence: a group of words that includes at least a verb/VP, Chapter 3, Section 2, and Chapter 7, Section 1.
S′	= S-bar: an S with a C added, see Chapter 7, Section 2.
S-adverbial	An adverbial that modifies the entire sentence or expresses the feelings of the speaker, e.g. *unfortunately,* as opposed to a VP-adverbial. See Chapter 5, Section 1.
SC	= Small Clause, see below.
sentence/clause	A unit that contains at least a verb. The subject may or may not be expressed, see Chapters 7, 8, and 10.
semantics	The linguistic aspects to meaning.
semi-modal	Auxiliary such as *dare (to), need (to), used to, ought to, have to.* They have properties of both main verbs and modal verbs, see Chapter 6, Section 1.1.
simple sentence/clause	sentence or clause with only one lexical verb, see Chapter 7.
sister	For example, a P and NP are sisters of each other; each has a branch going up to the 'mother', see Chapter 3, 1.1.
specify	Point to something, i.e. a determiner's function in a phrase.
split infinitive	Separating the *to* from the verb, e.g. as in *to boldly go …,* see special topic Chapter 5.
small clause	A sentence in which the verb has been left out, Chapter 4, Section 3.
stranding	Leaving the preposition behind, as in *the man I talked to,* see Chapter 10.
strong verbs	Term not used. Originally, a term for a verb that had a different vowel for the present, the past, and the past participle, e.g. *swim, swam, swum.* Now the terms is often used for any kind of irregular verb, e.g. *be, was, been.*
Su	=subject, see below.
subject	In English, the subject agrees with the verb in person and number, see Chapter 4, Section 1.1, and Table 4.1.
subject predicate	Often realized as an AdjP, making a claim about the subject, e.g. *nice* in *She is nice.* It occurs after a copula verb such as *be, become,* see Chapter 4, Section 1.3.
subjunctive	Expressing a wish or intention or necessity, e.g. *go* is a subjunctive verb in *it is important that he go there.* In Modern English, most of these are replaced by modal verbs, see Chapter 6, Section 1.1.

subordinate clause	Dependent clause, or clause embedded in another by means of a complementizer such as *that, because, if*, see Chapters 7 and 8.
subordinating conjunction	Not used in this book, same as complementizer, see there.
superlative	An adjective such as *greatest*, see Chapter 2.
synonym	A word with an almost identical meaning, e.g. *often* and *frequently*, Chapter 2.
syntax	Rules for how words are combined into phrases and sentences, the topic of this book, see Chapter 1.
t	= trace, see below
tag-question	A repetition of the subject and the auxiliary, as in *She has been there before, hasn't she?* See Chapter 4, Section 1.1.
tense	Indicating past or present time.
trace	Used to indicate that a word or phrase has been moved, a 'trace' is left in the original position, see Chapters 10 and 11.
transitive or monotransitive	Verb with one object, e.g. *see*, see Chapter 4, Section 2.
tree	A representation of the units/phrases of a sentence by means of branches and nodes, see Chapter 3.
two-part conjunction	Conjunction with two parts, e.g. *both Mary and John, neither Mary nor John*, Chapter 2.
Universal Grammar	Grammatical properties shared by all languages, see Chapter 1.
V	= verb
V′	= V-bar, an intermediate category, see Chapters 3 and 5.
verb	A lexical category often expressing a state, act, event or emotion, see Chapter 2, Section 1.1, and Table 2.1.
VGP	= Verb Group, see Chapter 6.
vowel	Sounds such as *i, e, a, o, u*, made by not blocking the airstream, see Chapter 1, 1.1. for use in a rule.
VP-adverbial	An adverbial that modifies the action of the verb, e.g. *quickly, slowly*, as opposed to an S-adverbial, see Chapter 5, Section 1.
wh-question	A question that starts with *who, what, how, why, when* or *where*, see Chapter 11, Section 1.2.
word order	Linear sequencing of words and phrases.
yes/no question	A question for which the appropriate answer would be 'yes', 'no', or 'maybe/perhaps', see Chapter 11, Section 1.1.
?	Questionable sentence.
*	Ungrammatical sentence.
^	May occur more than one.

1 Introduction

All of us know a lot about language. Most of the time, however, we are not conscious of this knowledge. When we actually study language, we attempt to find out what we know and how we acquire this linguistic knowledge. In this chapter, a number of instances will be given of what speakers of English intuitively know about the grammar of English, both about its sounds and its structure. The remainder of the book focusses on syntax, i.e. the categories and structures to account for our intuitive knowledge. The chapter also discusses social, i.e. non-linguistic, rules. These are often called prescriptive rules and some of these are dealt with as 'special topics' in this book.

1. Examples of linguistic knowledge

1.1 Consonants and vowels

If you are a native speaker of English, you know when to use the article *a* and when to use *an*. Speakers know how to do this correctly even though they might not be able to formulate the rule, which says that the article *a* occurs before a word that starts with a consonant, as in (1), and *an* occurs before a word that starts with a vowel, as in (2). If a child is given a nonsense word, as in (3), the child knows what form of the article to use:

1. a nice person, a treasure
2. an object, an artist
3. ovrite, cham

The rule for *a(n)* does not need to be taught explicitly in schools. It is only mentioned in connection with words that start with *h* or *u*. Since teachers are mainly worried about writing, they need to explain that what looks like a vowel in (4) is not in speech and that the *a/an* rule is based on speech. So, the form we choose depends on how the word is pronounced. In (4) and (6), the *u* and *h* are not pronounced as vowels but in (5) and (7), they are:

4. a union, a university
5. an uncle
6. a house, a hospital
7. an hour

The same rule predicts the pronunciation of *the* in (8). Pronounce the words in (8) and see if you can state the rule for the use of *the*:

8. The man, the table, the object, the hospital...

Examples (1) to (8) show the workings of a phonological (or sound) rule. The assumption is that we possess knowledge of consonants and vowels without having been taught the distinction. In fact, knowledge such as this enables us to learn the sound system of the language.

Apart from the structure of the sound system, also called phonology, a grammar will have to say something about the structure of words, or morphology. Native speakers are quite creative building words such as *kleptocracy, cyberspace, antidisestablishmentarianisms,* and even if you have never seen them before, knowing English means that you will know what these words mean based on their parts. Words such as *floccinaucinihilipilification,* meaning 'the categorizing of something as worthless or trivial', may be a little more difficult. This book will not be concerned with sound (phonology) or with the structure of words (morphology); it addresses how sentences are structured, often called syntax, or grammar, as in this book. In the next subsection, some examples are given of the syntactic knowledge native speakers possess.

1.2 Structure, auxiliaries, and movement

Each speaker of English has knowledge about the structure of a sentence. This is obvious from cases of ambiguity where sentences have more than one meaning. This often makes them funny. For instance, the headline in (9) is ambiguous in that 'cello case' can mean 'court case related to a cello', or 'someone called Cello', or 'a case to protect a cello':

9. Drunk Gets Ten Months In Cello Case.

In (9), the word 'case' is ambiguous (lexical ambiguity). The headlines in (10) to (12) are funny exactly because *drops, left, waffles, strikes* and *idle* can be ambiguous:

10. Eye drops off shelf.
11. British left waffles on Falkland Islands.
12. Teacher strikes idle kids.

Word ambiguities such as (10) to (12) are often produced on purpose for a certain effect, and are also called 'puns'. Some well-known instances from Lewis Carroll are the following:

> "Mine is a long and sad tale!" said the Mouse, turning to Alice and sighing. "It is a long tail, certainly," said Alice, looking with wonder at the Mouse's tail, "but why do you call it sad?"

> "How is bread made?" "I know that!" Alice cried eagerly. "You take some flour–" "Where do you pick the flower?" the White Queen asked. "In a garden, or in the hedges?" "Well, it isn't picked at all," Alice explained; "it's ground–" "How many acres of ground?" said the White Queen.

There are also sentences where the structure is ambiguous, e.g. (13), and the Hi & Lois Cartoon below it:

13. Speaker A: I just saw someone carrying a monkey and an elephant go into the circus.
    Speaker B: Wow, that someone must be pretty strong.

HI & LOIS

Reprinted with special permission of King Feature Syndicate.

The aim of this book is to understand the structure of English sentences; ambiguity is a major part of that, and in Chapter 3, more will be said about it.

Knowing about the structure is relevant in many cases, e.g. to ask a certain type of question, a verb is moved to the front of the sentence, as from (14) to (15):

14. The man is tall.
15. Is the man tall?

This rule is quite complex since we can't simply front any verb as (17) and (18), both derived from (16), show. In (17), the first verb of the sentence is fronted and this results in an ungrammatical sentence (indicated by the *); in (18), the second verb is fronted and this is grammatical:

16. The man who is in the garden is tall.
17. *Is the man who in the garden is tall?
18. Is the man who is in the garden tall?

These sentences show that speakers take the structure of a sentence into account when formulating questions (see also Chapter 3). We intuitively know that *the man who is in the garden* is a single unit and that the second verb is the one we need to move in order to make the question. This is not all, however. We also need to know that not all verbs move to form questions, as (19) shows. Only certain verbs, namely auxiliaries (see Chapter 6) and the verb *to be*, as in (15) and (18), are fronted:

19. *Arrived the bus on time?

In another kind of question, it is relevant to know what function the questioned word plays in the sentence. Thus, in (20) to (22), *who* is the object (see Chapter 4) of the verb *meet*. Without ever having been taught, we know that (22) is ungrammatical. With some trouble, we can figure out what (22) means. There is a story that Jane met someone and you believe this story. The speaker in (22) is asking who that someone is. Sentence (22) is ungrammatical because *who* moves 'too far'. It is possible, but not necessary here, to make precise what 'too far' means. The examples merely serve to show that speakers are aware of structure without explicit instruction and that *who* moves to the initial position:

20. Who did Jane meet?
21. Who did you believe that Jane met?
22. *Who did you believe the story that Jane met?

Some readers might object to the use of *who*, rather than *whom*, in (20) to (22). This use will be discussed in Chapter 10 and in the special topics to Chapters 4 and 10.

Thus, native speakers of English know that (a) sentences have a structure, e.g. (16), (b) movement occurs in questions, e.g. (16) and (20), and (c) verbs are divided into (at least) two kinds: verbs that move in questions (or auxiliary verbs) and verbs that don't move (or lexical verbs, as in (19)). More information on these three points will be given in Chapters 3, 11, and 6 respectively.

The other chapters deal with additional kinds of grammatical knowledge. Chapter 2 is about what we know regarding categories; Chapter 4 is about functions such as subject and object; Chapter 5 about adverbials; Chapter 9 about the structure of a phrase; and Chapters 7, 8 and 10 about the structure of more complex sentences.

2.   How do we know so much?

In Section 1, I discussed examples of what we know about language without being explicitly taught. How do we come by this knowledge? One theory that accounts for this was suggested by Noam Chomsky. He argues that we are all born with a language faculty that when "stimulated by appropriate and continuing experience, ... creates a grammar that creates sentences with formal and semantic properties" (1975: 36). Thus, our innate language faculty (or Universal Grammar) enables us to create a set of rules, or grammar, by being exposed to (generally rather chaotic) language around us. The set of rules that we acquire enables us to produce sentences we have never heard before. These sentences can also be infinitely long (if we had the time and energy). Language acquisition, in this framework, is not imitation but an interplay between Universal Grammar (UG) and exposure to a particular language.

This need for exposure to a particular language explains why, even though we all start out with the same UG, we acquire slightly different grammars. For instance, if you are exposed to a certain variety of Missouri or Canadian English, you might use (23); if exposed to a particular variety of British English, you might use (24); or, if exposed to a kind of American English, (25) and (26):

23.   I want for to go.
24.   You know as he left.
25.   She don't learn you nothing.
26.   Was you ever bit by a bee?

Thus, "[l]earning is primarily a matter of filling in detail within a structure that is innate" (Chomsky 1975: 39). "A physical organ, say the heart, may vary from one person to the next in size or strength, but its basic structure and its function within human physiology are common to the species. Analogously, two individuals in the same speech community may acquire grammars that differ somewhat in scale and subtlety... . [T]he products of the language faculty vary depending on triggering experience, ranging over the class of possible human languages (in principle). These variations in structure are limited, no doubt sharply, by UG" (p. 38).

Hence, even though Universal Grammar provides us with categories such as nouns and verbs that enable us to build our own grammars, the language we hear around us will determine the particular grammar we build up. A person from the 14th century who growing up has heard multiple negation, as in (27), would have a grammar that allows multiple negation. The same holds for a person from the 15th century who has heard (28). Please note that the original spelling has been kept in older examples. The Modern English equivalent, given in the single quotation marks, shows that we now need 'any' instead of another negative:

27.   Chaucer, *The Romaunt of the Rose*, l. 560–1
Men neded not in no cuntre
A fairer body for to seke.
'People did not need to seek a fairer person in any country'.

28.   *The Paston Letters*, letter 45 (1452), p. 71
for if he had he ne nedid not to haue sent no spyes.
'because if he had, he would not have needed to send any spies'.

Linguists typically say that one grammar is just as 'good' as any other. People may judge one variety as 'bad' and another as 'good', but for most people studying language, (23) through (26) are just interesting, not 'incorrect'. This holds for language change as well: the change from (27) and (28) to Modern English is not seen as either 'progress' or 'decay', but in more neutral terms.

Society also has rules, which I call social or 'non-linguistic', and which we need to take into account to be able to function. These are occasionally at odds with the (non-prescriptive) grammars speakers have in their heads. This is addressed in the next section.

3.   Examples of social or non-linguistic knowledge

We know when not to make jokes, for instance, when filling out tax forms or speaking with airport security people. We also know not to use words and expression such as *all you guys, awesome, I didn't get help from nobody* in formal situations such as applying for a job. We learn when and how to be polite and impolite; formal and informal. The rules for this differ from culture to culture and when we learn a new language, we also need to learn the politeness rules and rules for greetings, requests, etc.

When you are in informal situations (watching TV with a roommate), nobody will object to 'prescriptively proscribed' expressions, as in (29). In formal situations (testifying in court), you might use (30) instead:

29. I didn't mean nothin' by it.
30. I didn't intend to imply anything with that remark.

The differences between (29) and (30) involve many levels: vocabulary choice, e.g. *intend* rather than *mean*, phonology, e.g. *nothin*, and syntax, namely the double negative in (29). People use the distinction between formal and informal for 'effect' as well, as in (31):

31. You should be better prepared the next time you come to class. Ain't no way I'm gonna take this.

This book is not about the fight between descriptivism ('what people really say') and prescriptivism ('what some people think people ought to say'). As with all writing or speech, it makes a number of stylistic choices, e.g. use of contraction, use of 'I', the frequent use of passives, and avoidance of very long sentences. This, however, is irrelevant to the main point which is to provide the vocabulary and analytical skills to examine descriptive as well as prescriptive rules. The field that examines the status of prescriptive rules; regional forms as in (23) to (26); and formal and informal language, as in (31) to (30), is called sociolinguistics. Some prescriptive rules are analysed in the special topics sessions at the end of every chapter. The topics covered are adverbs used as adjectives and vice versa, multiple negation, as in (29), case marking (e.g. *It is me, between you and me*), split infinitives (*to boldly go where ...*), the use of *of* rather than *have* (*I should of done that*), subject-verb agreement, the preposition *like* used as a complementizer (*like I said ...*), dangling modifiers, and the 'correct' use of commas.

4. Conclusion

This first chapter has given instances of rules we know without having been taught, and offers an explanation about why we know this much (Universal Grammar 'helps' us). Other chapters in the book provide the categories and structures that we must be using to account for this intuitive knowledge. The chapter also provides instances of social or non-linguistic rules. These are often called prescriptive rules and some of these are dealt with as 'special topics' at the end of each of the chapters. The key terms in this chapter are **syntax; linguistic as** opposed to social or non-linguistic knowledge; descriptivism and prescriptivism; formal as opposed to informal language; innate faculty; and **Universal Grammar**.

Exercises

A. Can you give an instance of innate linguistic knowledge?

B. Do you think the following sentences are prescriptively correct or not. Why/why not?

32. It looks good.
33. Me and my friend went out.
34. Hopefully, hunger will be eliminated.
35. There's cookies for everyone.
36. Colorless green ideas sleep furiously.

Class discussion

C. Can you think of something you would say in an informal situation but not in a formal one?

D. Discuss in class why prescriptively 'correct' constructions are often used in formal situations.

E. You may have heard of best-selling 'language mavens' such as William Safire or Edwin Newman. Safire is a political commentator who also writes a weekly column in the Sunday *New York Times*. Titles of his books include *Good Advice, I Stand Corrected: More on Language,* and *Language Maven Strikes Again.* Newman, a former NBC correspondent, writes books entitled *A Civil Tongue* and *Strictly Speaking.* These lead reviewers to say "Read Newman! Save English before it is fatally slain" (from the backcover).

Discuss where you think these gurus or mavens get their authority.

F. Explain the ambiguity in (37) to (39):

37. light house keeper.
38. old dogs and cats.
39. Herma gave her dog biscuits.

Keys to the Exercises

A. Consonants and vowels: all languages have them and we use them in building our linguistic rules.

B. – (32) is correct since *good* is an adjective giving more information about the pronoun *it* (see Chapter 2 and special topic).
    – (33) is not since the subject should get nominative case (see Chapter 4 and special topic).
    – (34) is not since *hopefully* is not supposed to be used as a sentence adverb (see Chapter 5 and special topic of Chapter 2).
    – (35) is not since the verb is singular (*is*) and the subject is plural (*cookies*). This violates subject-verb agreement (see Chapter 4 and special topic to Chapter 9).
    – (36) is Noam Chomsky's famous sentence. It is perfectly grammatical and shows that syntax and grammar are separate from meaning.

2   Categories

In this chapter, I provide descriptions of the main lexical categories: Noun, Verb, Adjective, Adverb, and Preposition. These categories are called lexical because they carry meaning (have synonyms and antonyms) and, as we'll see in the next chapter, they are the heads of phrases. There are also functional or grammatical categories: Determiner, Auxiliary, Coordinator, and Complementizer. These categories are called grammatical or functional categories since they do not contribute to the meaning of a sentence but determine the syntax of it. They do not function as heads of phrases but merely as parts or as connectors. I'll refer to them as grammatical categories. Prepositions and adverbs are a little of both as will be explained in Sections 1.2 and 1.3 respectively, as are pronouns, e.g. *it, she, there*, which is discussed in Section 3.

When languages borrow new words, these will mainly be nouns, verbs, and adjectives, i.e. lexical categories. Therefore, the difference between lexical and grammatical is often put in terms of open as opposed to closed categories, the lexical categories being open (new words can be added) and the grammatical ones being closed (new words are not easily added). Section 4 will examine that in a limited way.

1.   Lexical categories

The five lexical categories are Noun, Verb, Adjective, Adverb, and Preposition. They carry meaning, and often words with a similar (synonym) or opposite meaning (antonym) can be found. Frequently, the noun is said to be a person, place, or thing and the verb is said to be an event or act. These are semantic definitions. In this chapter, it is shown that semantic definitions are not completely sufficient and that we need to define categories syntactically (according to what they combine with) and morphologically (according to how the words are formed). For example, syntactically speaking, *chair* is a noun because it combines with the article (or determiner) *the*; morphologically speaking, *chair* is a noun because it takes a plural ending as in *chairs*.

1.1 Nouns (N) and Verbs (V)

A noun generally indicates a person, place or thing (i.e. this is its meaning). For instance, *chair, table*, and *book* are nouns since they refer to things. However, if the distinction between a noun as person, place or thing and a verb as an event or action were the only distinction, certain nouns such as *action* and *destruction* would be verbs, since they imply action. These elements are nevertheless seen as nouns. Thus, in (1) and (2), *actions* and *destruction* are preceded by the article *the*, are followed by a phrase starting with a preposition, can be pluralized with an *-s*, and occur in sentences with verbs (*came* and *caused*). As will be shown in Chapter 4, their functions in the sentence are also typical for nouns rather than verbs: in (1), *actions* is part of the subject, and in (2), *destruction* is part of the object:

1. The actions by the government came too late.
2. The hurricane caused the destruction of the villages.

Apart from plural *-s*, other morphological characteristics of nouns are shown in (3) and (4). Possessive *'s* (or genitive case) appears only on nouns, e.g. *Jenny* in (3), and affixes such as *-er* and *-ism*, e.g. *writer* and *postmodernism* in (4), are also typical for nouns:

3. Jenny's neighbor always knows the answer.
4. That writer has modernized postmodernism.

Syntactic reasons for calling nouns nouns are that nouns are often preceded by *the*, as in (1), (2), and (3), or *that*, as in (4); and that if they are followed by another noun, there has to be a preposition, such as *by* in (1) and *of* in (2), connecting them.

The nouns *action* and *destruction* have verbal counterparts, namely *act* and *destroy*, and (1) and (2) can be paraphrased as (5) and (6) respectively:

5. The government acted too late.
6. The hurricane destroyed the villages.

Just as nouns cannot always be defined as people or things, verbs are not always acts, even though *acted* and *destroyed* are. For instance, *is*, a form of the verb *be* in (7), does not express an action. Hence, we need to add state to the semantic definition of verb, as well as emotion to account for sentences such as (8):

7. The book is red and blue.
8. The book seemed nice (to me).

Some of the morphological characteristics of verbs are that they can express tense, e.g. past in (5), (6), and (8) and present in (7); that the verb ends in -*s* when it has a third person singular subject (see Chapter 4) and is present tense; and that it may have an affix typical for verbs, namely -*ize*, e.g. in *modernized* in (4) (note that it is -*ise* in British English). Syntactically, they can be followed by a noun, as in (6), rather than by a preposition and a noun, as in (2), or they can be preceded by an auxiliary, as in (4). Some of the major differences between nouns and verbs are summarized in Table 2.1 below.

In English, nouns can easily be used as verbs and verbs as nouns. Therefore, it is necessary to look at the context in which a word occurs, as in (9), for example, where Shakespeare uses *vnckle*, i.e. 'uncle', as a verb as well as a noun:

9. Shakespeare, *Richard II*, II, 3, 96 (First Folio edition)
    York: Grace me no Grace, nor Vnckle me,
    I am no Traytors Vnckle; and that word Grace
    In an vngracious mouth, is but prophane.

Thus, using the criteria discussed above, the first instance of 'uncle' would be a verb since the noun following it does not need to be connected to the verb by means of a preposition, and the second 'uncle' is a noun since 'traitor' has the possessive *'s*. Note that Shakespeare's spelling, punctuation, and grammar are far from 'regularized'.

Other examples where a word can be both a noun and a verb are *table, to table; chair, to chair; floor, to floor; book, to book; fax, to fax; telephone, to telephone*; and *walk, to walk*. Some of these started out as nouns and some as verbs. For instance, *fax* is the shortened form of the noun *facsimile* but is now used as a verb as well. An often-used sentence where *police* is used as noun, verb, and adjective respectively is (10):

10. Police police police outing.

As we'll see, other words can be ambiguous in this way.

As a summary to Section 1.1, I provide a table. Morphological differences involve the shape of an element while syntactic ones involve how the element fits in a sentence. The semantic differences involve meaning, but remember to be careful here since nouns, for instance, can have verbal meanings as in (1) and (2) above.

Table 2.1. Some differences between N and V

	Noun	Verb
Morphology	a. plural -s with a few exceptions, e.g. *children, deer, mice*	h. past tense -ed with a few exceptions, e.g. *went, left*
	b. possessive *'s*	i. third person singular agreement -s
	c. some end in *-ity, -ness, -ation, -er, -ion, -ment*	j. some end in *-ize,-ate*
Syntax	d. preceded by *the/a* and *this/that/ these/those*	k. preceded by an auxiliary e.g. *have*
	e. modified by adjective	l. modified by adverb
	f. followed by preposition and noun	m. can be followed by noun
Semantics	g. person, place, thing	n. act, event, state, emotion

Differences (e) and (l) have not been commented on in this section, but will be explained in the next. As a transition, I provide (11), where the adjective *expensive* modifies (i.e. says something about) the noun *book*, whereas the adverb *quickly* modifies the verb *sold out*:

11. That expensive book sold out quickly.

1.2 Adjectives and Adverbs

Adverbs and Adjectives are semantically very similar in that both modify another element, i.e. they describe a quality of another word: *quick/ly, nice/ly*, etc. As just mentioned, the main syntactic distinction is as expressed in (12):

12. An adjective modifies a noun;
     an adverb modifies a verb, and (a degree adverb) modifies an adjective, or adverb.

Since an adjective modifies a noun, the quality it describes will be one appropriate to a noun, e.g. nationality (*American, Navajo, Dutch, Iranian*), size (*big, large, thin*), color (*red, yellow, blue*), or character trait (*happy, fortunate, lovely, pleasant, obnoxious*). Adverbs typically modify actions and will then provide information typical of those, e.g. manner (*wisely, fast*), or duration (*frequently, often*), or speaker attitude (*fortunately*), or place (*there, abroad*), or time (*then*). *As well* and *also*, and negatives such as *not* and *never* are also adverbs.

When adverbs modify adjectives or other adverbs, they are typically degree adverbs (*very, so, too*). These degree adverbs have very little meaning and it is hard to find synonyms or antonyms. It therefore makes more sense to consider this subgroup of adverbs grammatical categories.

Some instances of the 'correct' use of the adjective *nice* are given in (13) and (14) and of the adverbs *very* and *quickly* in (15) and (16):

13. The book is nice.
14. A nice book is on the table.
15. This Hopi bowl is very precious.
16. He drove very quickly.

In (13) and (14), *nice* modifies the noun *book*. In (15), *very* modifies the adjective *precious*; and in (16), it modifies the adverb *quickly*, which in its turn modifies the verb *drove*. (We will come back to some of the issues related to the precise nature of the modification in Chapters 3, 4, and 9). In the 'special topic' section at the end of this chapter, it will be shown that speakers often violate rule (12), but that these so-called violations are rule-governed as well.

Generally speaking, an adverb is formed from an adjective by adding -*ly*, as in (15) and (16). However, be careful with this morphological distinction: not all adverbs end in -*ly* and some adjectives end in -*ly*. If you are uncertain as to whether a word is an adjective or an adverb, either look in a dictionary to see what the correct form is, or use it in a sentence to see what it modifies. For instance, *fast, hard, low* are both adjectives and adverbs. In (17), *fast* is an adjective because it modifies a noun, but in (18), it is an adverb since it modifies a verb:

17. That fast car must be a police car.
18. That car drives fast.

In a number of cases, words such as *hard* and *fast* can be either adjectives or adverbs, depending on the interpretation. In (19), *hard* can either modify the noun *person*, i.e. the person looks tough or nasty, in which case it is an adjective, or it can modify *look* (meaning that the person was looking all over the place for something, i.e. the effort was great) in which case *hard* is an adverb:

19. That person looked hard.

A last point to make about adjectives and adverbs is that most (if they are gradable) can be used to compare or contrast two or more things. We call such forms the comparative (e.g. *better than*) or superlative (e.g. *the best*). One way to make these forms is to add *-er/-est*, as in *nicer/nicest*. Not all adjectives/ adverbs allow this ending, however; some need to be preceded by *more/most*, as in *more intelligent, most intelligent*. Sometimes, people are creative with comparatives and superlatives, especially in advertising, as in (20) and (21), or in earlier forms as in (22):

20. mechanic: 'the expensivest oil is ...'.
21. advertizement: 'the bestest best ever phone'.
22. Shakespeare, *King Lear* II, 3, 7
     To take the basest and most poorest shape ...

There are also irregular comparative and superlative forms, such as *good, better, best; bad, worse, worst*. These have to be learned as exceptions to the rules, and can be played with, as in the pun 'When I am bad, I am better'.

To summarize this section, I'll provide a table listing differences between adjectives and adverbs.

Table 2.2. Differences between adjectives and adverbs

	Adjectives		Adverbs	
Morphology	a.	no *-ly* in most cases	d.	end in *-ly* in many cases (exceptions *fast, now*)
Syntax	b.	modify N	e.	modify V, Adj, or Adv
Semantics	c.	describe qualities typical of nouns, e.g: nationality, color, size.	f.	qualities of verbs, e.g: place, manner, time, duration, etc. and of adjectives/adverbs: degree

1.3 Prepositions

Prepositions often express place or time (*at, in, on, before*), direction (*to, from, into, down*), or relation (*of, about, with, like, as, near*). They are invariable in form and occur before a noun (or Noun Phrase, see the next chapter), as (23) shows, where the prepositions are in bold:

23. **With** their books **about** linguistics, they went **to** school.

On occasion, 'prepositions' are used on their own, as in (24). In such cases, they are considered adverbs or particles (see Chapter 5), not prepositions. The difference between prepositions and adverbs is that prepositions come before the nouns they relate to, e.g. *their books, linguistics,* and *school* in (23) belong to *with, about,* and *to* respectively. Infrequently, prepositions are used as verbs, as in (25):

24. He went in; they ran out; he jumped up.
25. They upped the price.

Some other examples of prepositions are *during, around, after, against, despite, except, without, towards, until, till, inside.* Sequences such as *instead of, outside of, away from, due to* and *as for* are also considered to be prepositions, even though they consist of two words.

Some prepositions have very little lexical meaning and are mainly used for grammatical purposes. For instance, *of* in (26) expresses a relationship between two nouns rather than a meaning:

26. The door of that car.

Prepositions are therefore a category with lexical and grammatical characteristics. Here, however, I will treat them as lexical, for the sake of simplicity.

2. Grammatical categories

The main grammatical categories are Determiner, Auxiliary, Coordinator, and Complementizer. As also mentioned above, it is hard to define grammatical categories in terms of meaning because they have very little. Their function is to make the lexical categories fit together.

2.1 Determiner

The determiner category includes the articles *a(n)* and *the,* as well as demonstratives, possessive pronouns, possessive nouns, some quantifiers, some interrogatives, and some numerals. So, determiner (or D) is an umbrella term for all of these. Determiners occur with a noun to specify which noun is meant or whose it is. Examples of *a(n)* and *the* are given in (13) and (14) above. There are four demonstratives in English: *this, that, these,* and *those,* and an example occurs in (17) above.

Possessive pronouns include *my, your, his, her, its, our,* and *their,* as in (27). Nouns can be possessives as well, but in that case they have an - *'s* (or *'*) ending, as in (28):

27. Their kangaroo ate my food.

28. Bor's food was eaten by Pim.

In (27), *their* and *my* specify whose kangaroo and whose food it was, and in (28) the possessive noun *Bor's* specifies whose food was eaten.

Determiners as in (27) and (28) precede nouns just like adjectives, but whereas a determiner points out which entity is meant (it specifies), an adjective describes the quality (it modifies). When both a determiner and an adjective precede a noun, the determiner always precedes the adjective, as in (29), and not the other way round, as in (30) (indicated by the asterisk). In Chapter 9, this order will be elaborated on:

29. Their irritating dog ate my delicious food.

30. *Irritating their dog ate delicious my food.

Interrogatives such as *whose* in *whose books*, *what* in *what problems*, and *which* in *which computer* are determiners. Quantifiers such as *any*, *many*, *much*, and *all* are usually considered determiners, e.g. in *much work*, *many people*, and *all research*. Some are used before other determiners, namely, *all*, *both*, and *half*, as in (31). These quantifiers are called pre-determiners, and abbreviated Pre-D. Finally, quantifiers may be adjectival, as in *the many problems* and in (32):

31. All the books; half that wealthy man's money; both those problems.

32. The challenges are many/few.

Numerals are sometimes determiners, as in *two books*, and sometimes more like adjectives, as in *my two books*. Table 2.3 shows the determiners in the order in which they may appear. I have added Adjective to the table since some of the words that are clear determiners can also be adjectives. The categories are not always perfectly clear-cut.

Table 2.3. Determiners

	Pre-D	D	Adj
quantifier	all, both half	some, many, all, few any, much, every, etc.	many, few
article		the, a	
demonstrative		that, this, those, these	
possessive		my, etc., NP's	
interrogative		whose, what, which, etc	
numeral		one, two, etc.	one, two, etc.

2.2 Auxiliary

This category will be dealt with in detail in Chapter 6. For now, it suffices to say that, as its name implies, the auxiliary functions to help another verb, but does not itself contribute greatly to the meaning of the sentence. Verbs such as *have, be,* and *do* can be full verbs, as in (33), or auxiliaries, as in (34). In (34), *have* does not mean 'possess' or 'hold', but contributes to the grammatical meaning of the sentence, namely past tense with present relevance. The same is true for *be* in (35); it contributes to the grammatical meaning emphasizing the continuous nature of the event:

33.   I have a book in my hand.
34.   I have worked here for 5 years.
35.   Santa may be working Thanksgiving Day.

Because auxiliaries help other verbs (except when they are main verbs as in (33)), they cannot occur on their own, as in (36), which is ungrammatical:

36.   *I must a book.

2.3 Coordinator and Complementizer

Coordinators such as *and* and *or* join two elements of the same kind, e.g. the nouns in (37). They are also sometimes called coordinating conjunctions, but in this book, we'll use coordinator. There are also two-part coordinators such as *both ... and, either ... or,* and *neither ... nor.*

Complementizers such as *that, because, whether, if,* and *since* are also called subordinating conjunctions or subordinators. We will use complementizer. They join two clauses where one clause is subordinate to the other (see Chapter 7 for more), as in (38):

37.   Rigobertha and Pablo went to Madrid and Barcelona.
38.   Rigobertha and Pablo left because Sunny was about to arrive.

Like prepositions, coordinators and complementizers are invariable, i.e. never have an ending, in English.

There is a group of words, namely *yet, however, nevertheless, therefore,* and *so,* as in (39), that connects one sentence to another:

39.   Jane Austen, Emma, Vol 1, chap 8
      "you are anxious for a compliment, so I will tell you that you have improved her".

Some grammarians see these as complementizers; others see them as adverbs. With the punctuation as in (39), the complementizer scenario is more obvious since *so* connects the two sentences. However, *so* sometimes appears at the beginning of a sentence, in which case it could be an adverb expressing the reason why something was done. I leave it up to you to decide what to do with these. Remember from Section 1.2 that *so* can also be a degree adverb, as in *so nice*.

3.   Pronouns

Personal pronouns, such as *I, me, she, he* and *it*, are seen as grammatical categories by many. The reason is that they don't mean very much: they are used to refer to phrases already mentioned. However, in this book, I classify personal pronouns as nouns, since they very much function like full Noun Phrases (more on this in the next chapter). Thus, a determiner such as *the* cannot stand on its own, but *she*, as in (40) from Shakespeare, can:

40.   *Hamlet*, IV, 5, 14
       'Twere good **she** were spoken with,
       For **she** may strew dangerous coniectures
       in ill breeding minds.

Because pronouns stand on their own, and can function as subjects or objects (see Chapter 4 for more), I treat pronouns as lexical.

The pronouns can be divided according to number into singular and plural and according to person into first, second, and third person. For example, *I* and *me* are first person singular, and *we* and *us* are first person plural. The second person pronoun *you* is used both as singular and as plural. Third person singular pronouns *he, she,* and *it* are further divided according to gender, but the third person plural *they* is not.

Taking the argument of independence seriously, almost all determiners, except the articles can stand on their own, e.g. demonstratives, such as *that* in *that is a problem*. The same is true for possessive pronouns that occur on their own, and are therefore not determiners. Examples are *mine, yours, his, hers, ours,* and *theirs*, as in (41):

41.   That e-mail is not mine, but it is yours.

These pronouns appear when the noun they specify has been left unspecified. Thus, (41) could be rewritten as (42), with *mine* replaced by *my e-mail*. The result is awkward, however, and therefore I will argue *mine* and *yours* are really independent pronouns, not determiners with the noun left out:

42.   That e-mail is not my e-mail, but it is your e-mail.

The other determiners, namely interrogatives, quantifiers, and numerals can be used on their own as well, as in (43). It will be up to the reader to decide whether these are independent pronouns or are really determiners preceding nouns that have been left out (through ellipsis):

43.   **What** would be solved if **all** chose **two?**

4.   What new words and loanwords tell us

Some of the new words of the 20th century are *pizza, angst, fax, e-mail, phat, AIDS, website, browser, screenager, to surf, Nethead, infomaze, e-zine, gopher, ….,* to name but a few, and they are all lexical categories! Some of these are loan-words (*angst* from German), some are extensions of other meanings (*surf the net* from *surf the waves*), some are clipped (*electronic-magazine* becomes *e-zine*), others come from special cultures (e.g. *phat*, meaning 'desirable, cool'), but all are lexical, rather than grammatical categories.

Lewis Carroll's *Jabberwocky* includes a number of 'nonsense' words. As an exercise, at the end of the chapter, you'll be asked what category each of these is. For now, it is enough to point out that they are all lexical:

'Twas brillig, and the slithy toves
Did gyre and gimble in the wabe:
All mimsy were the borogoves
And the mome raths outgrabe.

"Beware the Jabberwock, my son!
The jaws that bite, the claws that catch!
Beware the Jubjub bird and shun
The frumious Bandersnatch!"

He took his vorpal sword in hand:
Longtime the manxome foe he sought –
So rested he by the Tumtum tree
And stood a while in thought. (...)

There are other phenomena that the lexical/grammatical distinction sheds light on. For instance, children learn lexical categories before grammatical ones, and aphasics can have difficulties with either lexical or grammatical categories (see Exercise D below). So there is empirical (from the outside world) evidence for the distinction made in this chapter.

5. Conclusion

The categories discussed in this chapter are defined in semantic, morphological, and syntactic terms, i.e. according to meaning, word-form, and position in the sentence. An important concept for classifying determiners is **specify** (or point to) and one for classifying adjectives and adverbs is **modify** (or describe the quality of).

The key terms in this chapter are **lexical category (Noun, Verb, Adjective, Adverb, Preposition** and **Pronoun)** and **grammatical category (Determiner, Quantifier, Auxiliary, Coordinator** and **Complementizer)**, or **open** as opposed to **closed.**

Exercises

A. Make a sentence
   (a) where an adjective modifies a noun,
   (b) where an adverb modifies an adjective,
   (c) where an adverb modifies another adverb and the two together modify a verb.

B. Identify each word in the text below. Some words are problematic, e.g. *last.*

> At last, we had begun filming. Should I say 'we'? I was living in the house and extremely curious about everything connected with the film. Fortunately, they let me hang around and even gave me a job. As an historian, I kept an eye on detail and did not allow the filmmakers to stray too far from the period of Louis Philippe. The project was to make an hour-long film about Houdin and it was decided to shoot the picture in Switzerland. This may have been a bad idea. It certainly mixed professional and domestic affairs.
>
> (adapted from *World of Wonders*, R. Davies, I, 2)

C. To what categories do the nonsense words belong in Lewis Carroll's "Jabberwocky", given in Section 4 above? Discuss in class why you chose those categories.

D. Broca's aphasia results in a loss of grammatical categories, such as determiners and auxiliaries, but not the loss of lexical categories, such as nouns and verbs. It is sometimes called agrammatism. Wernicke's aphasia results in a loss of meaning, but not in a loss of grammatical categories. Which sentence exemplifies which aphasia?

    I.   I could if I can help these like this you know ... to make it.

    II. Well ... front ... soldiers ... campaign ... soldiers ... to shoot ... well ... head ... wound ... and hospital ... and so ...

    (from O'Grady et al. 1987)

E. Discuss the syntactic use (i.e. which category is modified) of adjectives and adverbs in the following excerpts:

(a) the first line of Roethke's *Villanelle* 'I wake to sleep and take my waking slow', of which only the first 6 lines are given.

    The Waking

    I wake to sleep and take my waking slow.
    I feel my fate in what I cannot fear.
    I learn by going where I have to go.

    We think by feeling. What is there to know?
    I hear my being dance from ear to ear.
    I wake to sleep and take my waking slow.

    ...

(b) parts of D. H. Lawrence's *Snake*

    Snake

    A snake came to my water-trough
    On a hot, hot day, and I in pyjamas for the heat,
    To drink there.

    In the deep, strange-scented shade of the great dark carob-tree
    I came down the steps with my pitcher
    And must wait, must stand and wait, for there he was at the trough before me.

    ...

And voices in me said, If you were a man
You would take a stick and break him now, and finish him off.

But must I confess how I liked him,
How glad I was he had come like a guest in quiet, to drink at my water-trough
And depart peaceful, pacified, and thankless,
Into the burning bowels of this earth?

...

F. Most people, if asked to provide or repeat the first line of Dylan Thomas'
poem below, will say 'Do not go gently ...' with *gently* as an adverb modifying the verb. Why is *gentle* grammatical as well?

Do Not Go Gentle into That Good Night,

Do not go gentle into that good night,
Old rage should burn and rave at close of day;
Rage, rage against the dying of the light.

Though wise men at their end know dark is right,
Because their words had forked no lightning they
Do not go gentle into that good night

Good men, the last wave by, crying how bright
Their frail deeds might have danced in a green bay,
Rage, rage against the dying of the light.

Wild men who caught and sang the sun in flight,
And learn, too late, they grieved it on its way,
Do not go gentle into that good night.

G. Take 5 words that are grammatical categories and look them up in a dictionary
(e.g. the *American Heritage Dictionary* at www.bartleby.com/61/). How do
dictionaries deal with them?

Class discussion

H. Identify the categories of every word in Wallace Stevens' 'Anecdote of the
Jar', i.e. N, V, Adj, Adv, P, Det, AUX, C, and Pronoun. Are there any words
that you are unsure about? Make an educated guess as to their category.

I placed a jar in Tennessee,
And round it was, upon a hill.

It made the slovenly wilderness
Surround that hill.

The wilderness rose up to it,
And sprawled around, no longer wild.
The jar was round upon the ground
And tall and of a port in air.
It took dominion everywhere.
The jar was grey and bare.
It did not give of bird or bush,
Like nothing else in Tennessee.

I. In class, it has been argued that lexical categories can be borrowed from one language into another (e.g. karaoke, taco, sauerkraut) or 'invented' (e-mail, chat-room, web navigator). Can you think of a preposition or a pronoun that has been borrowed or made up? What does your answer mean for the status (lexical/grammatical) of these categories?

J. Briefly discuss the poem 'We Real Cool' by Gwendolyn Brooks in the light of either Chapter 1 or 2 or both:

We real cool. We
Left school. We

Lurk Late. We
Strike straight. We

Sing sin. We
Thin gin. We

Jazz June. We
Die soon.

K. Do the same for the following sentences taken from Shakespeare:

44. Ile serve thee true and faithfully till then. (Love's Labor's Lost, V, 2, 840)
45. Thou didst it excellent (Taming of the Shrew, I, 1, 89)
46. Tis Noble Spoken (Anthony and Cleopatra, II, 2, 99)

Keys to the Exercises

A. a.   The **nice** computer crashed.
         That was not **pleasant**.
         He is this very **abrasive** politician.

    b.   He is this **very** abrasive lawyer.
         That was **extraordinarily** irritating.
         The **extremely** unpleasant judge was impeached.

    c.   I can see **very** well from here.
         He drove **extremely** quickly.
         The officer said that she drove **too** fast.

B. In the key, I have identified every word, but the difference between verb (V)
    and auxiliary (AUX) will only become clear in Chapter 6. I have also
    identified Coord(inators) and D(eterminers). Note that I classify pronouns
    as N, but you could classify them as pronoun (or Pron) if you want to:

    At (P) last (Adj), we (N) had (AUX) begun (V) filming (V). Should (AUX)
    I (N) say (V) 'we' (N)? I (N) was (AUX) living (V) in (P) the (D) house (N)
    and (Coord) extremely (Adv) curious (Adj) about (P) everything (N)
    connected (V) with (P) the (D) film (N). Fortunately (Adv), they (N) let
    (V) me (N) hang (V) around (Adv) and (Coord) even (Adv) gave (V) me
    (N) a (D) job (N). As (P) an (D) historian (N), I (N) kept (V) an (D) eye
    (N) on (P) detail (N) and (Coord) did (AUX) not (Adv) allow (V) the (D)
    filmmakers (N) to (AUX, see Chapter 6) stray (V) too (Adv) far (Adv) from
    (P) the (D) period (N) of (P) Louis (N) Philippe (N). The (D) project (N)
    was (V) to (AUX) make (V) an (D) hour-long (Adj) film (N) about (P)
    Houdin (N) and (Coord) it (N) was (AUX) decided (V) to (AUX) shoot
    (V) the (D) picture (N) in (P) Switzerland (N). This (N) may (AUX) have
    (AUX) been (V) a (D) bad (Adj) idea (N). It (N) certainly (Adv) mixed (V)
    professional (Adj) and (Coord) domestic (Adj) affairs (N).

C. 'Twas brillig (Adj), and the slithy (Adj) toves (N)
    Did gyre (V) and gimble (V) in the wabe (N):
    All mimsy (Adj) were the borogoves (N)
    And the mome (Adj/N ?) raths (N) outgrabe (V).

    "Beware the Jabberwock (N), my son!
    The jaws that bite, the claws that catch!

Beware the Jubjub (Adj/N) bird and shun
The frumious (Adj) Bandersnatch!"

He took his vorpal (Adj) sword in hand:
Longtime the manxome (Adj) foe he sought –
So rested he by the Tumtum (Adj/N) tree
And stood a while in thought. (…)

D. I is Wernicke; II is Broca.

E. Roethke's 'I wake to sleep and take my waking slow' is puzzling since if the poet really wanted to sleep, he should not want to be slow in falling asleep. There is a symmetry in the two sentences in that both start with similar sounding verbs (*wake* and *take*) and the first verb is repeated (*waking*). This focusses our attention on the waking and yet the author purports to be interested in sleeping. As to the use of adjectives, only one is used (*slow*) and, on first reading, we might think this is incorrect and that it has to be an adverb (*slowly*). It is not incorrect and, moreover, using the adjective rather than the adverb focusses our attention on *waking* rather than on the verb *take*.

Lawrence's *Snake* is about reflection and lack of action. It describes a still, beautiful scene, which is emphasized by the use of adjectives such as *hot* (l. 2) and *deep, strange-scented, great,* and *dark* (l. 4). There is also a conflict between the peace of the moment (and nature) and the voices (of education, etc.). The conflict is emphasized by the use of the adjectives *peaceful, pacified, thankless* as opposed to *burning*. It is the snake that is seen as peaceful, hence, *depart peaceful* and not *depart peacefully*.

F. Grammatically speaking, having an adverb such as *gently* modify *go* is not incorrect. Dylan Thomas' version, however, is very different. By using the adjective form *gentle*, another interpretation becomes available, one where the person addressed in the poem should not 'become gentle'. Now, because of its form, *gentle* modifies the implied 'you'. The effect is very different.

G. If you look some up in a dictionary that is historically based (e.g. the Oxford English Dictionary), you will run into trouble because there is so much information. For instance, *the* is listed as 'demonstrative', 'pronoun', and 'article'. A less historical dictionary might just give 'article'.

Special topic: Adverb and Adjective

The rule stated in (12) above is often ignored by native speakers. In its simple form, it reads: an adjective modifies a noun; an adverb modifies a verb, adjective or adverb. The reason that the rule is not always followed is that the language is changing. For instance, *real* is a degree adverb, and becoming more like other degree adverbs such as *too, so, very* that lack the *-ly* ending. In (13) to (18) above, examples of the 'correct' use of adjectives and adverbs are given. Some additional ones are listed here in (47) to (52), where the adjective modifies a noun:

47. Lawrence Durrell, *Sebastian*, p. 12
    She waited impassive.
48. I made it in safe.
49. I list them separate.
50. He tested positive.
51. *The Mesa Tribune*, 29 August 1996, A1
    In an article on nails: 'Color them unusual'.
52. *The Mesa Tribune*, 15 February 1999, A1
    911 system stretched thin.

Explain what the adjectives in (47) to (52) modify. In these sentences, it is possible to add a *-ly* and make the adjective into an adverb. Then, the meaning changes since now the adverb modifies the verb. Can you do that?

Examples of 'incorrect use' are listed in (53) to (56). Explain why they are prescriptively incorrect:

53. Judge in Texas (quoted in the NYT, 30 August 1995, A9)
    'because if she doesn't do good in school, then …'.
54. In formal speech:
    You did that real good.
55. It looks beautifully.
56. Does the clutch feel any differently? (The Tappet Brothers on 'Car Talk')

These sentences illustrate three problems speakers encounter. Firstly, as mentioned, *really* is losing its ending when it is degree adverb, as in (54). As Swan (1980: 12) writes: "In informal conversational English (especially American English), *real* is often used instead of *really* before adjectives and adverbs". Note that nobody uses *real* in (57). Why might that be the case?

57. Really, you shouldn't have done that.

Secondly, the adverb counterpart to the adjective *good* is not *good*, as in (53) and (54), or *goodly*, but *well*, as in (58), the rewritten version of (54). *Well* is also used as adjective, as in (59). It is no wonder speakers become confused! In (59), *good* can replace *well*. Please explain why:

58. You did that really well.
59. I am well, thank you.

Thirdly, speakers tend to overreact when they see an adjective next to a verb, and hypercorrect themselves. Hypercorrection occurs when speakers are so unsure that they think about the prescriptive rule too much and confuse themselves. They think that if an adjective is next to a verb, it has to modify the verb and be an adverb, as in (55) and (56). The poem by Dylan Thomas cited above shows, however, that this is not always necessary. Hypercorrection, as in (56), is different from a change such as in (54).

As a last point, a comment on *hopefully* is necessary. Swan (1980: 296–7) mentions that there are two uses: one is full of hope, as in (60), and the other use, as in (61), "shows the speaker's attitude", and means it is hoped. According to Swan, "[s]ome people consider the second use 'incorrect'. Both functions will be dealt with in Chapter 5:

60. She sat there hopefully for someone to stop by.
61. Hopefully, hunger will cease to be a problem.

It is not clear why *hopefully* should have attracted all this attention. There are several other adverbs like it, e.g. those in (62) to (65):

62. Naturally, I'd like you to stay with us for a few days.
63. Amazingly, he arrived on time.
64. Fortunately, the bus wasn't late.
65. Funnily enough, I'd been thinking about that.

In (62) to (65), the adverbs all express the speaker's attitude and this is a legitimate use of an adverb; they do not all have to modify the VP. More on this in Chapter 5.

The head of a)
The word the pharse is built around is
Called the head. (31)

The lines, called branches indicate
how the pharse is divided up.

Branches come together in "nodes".

The node in between the (NP) and N is
Called N' pronounced N-bar

a way to figure out what noun is the
head 1. Shorten Sentence, you can use pro- N

ex. The unpleasant unicorn from mac love Dogfood
✗ The unicorn Loves dogfood 2. what parts modify

N. Head.
The nodes are usually labeled N, N' or NP
N' is intermediate between the top NP and
the N. Such Allow one to know which Elements
are grouped together. 32

The Adj. ph indicate properties of
Nouns. The AdvP are built around Adv
Which indicate qualities of Verbs (34)

degree marker Such as very, too, extremely +
really. In a Adverb P they act as (D) ob
They do no branch out to make a pharse
of their own. Pg35

VP indicate action They contain other pharses
NP, PP, + Adj Indicate what, where, when why how
" PP always Contains a P + a noun phar
(Page 40) (Page 43) 3. 1 44 + 45

3   Phrases

Sentences can be divided into groups of words that belong together. For instance, in *the nice unicorn ate a delicious meal*, *the*, *nice*, and *unicorn* form one such group and *a*, *delicious*, and *meal* form another. (We all know this intuitively). The group of words is called a phrase. If the most important part of the phrase, i.e. the head, is an adjective, the phrase is an Adjective Phrase; if the most important part of the phrase is a noun, the phrase is a Noun Phrase, and so on. One could indicate phrases by putting brackets around them, but that gets confusing if the sentence is complex, and as an alternative, 'trees' are used. Trees render the structure of the sentence clearer and less ambiguous. The grammatical categories (Determiner, Auxiliary, Coordinator, and Complementizer) do not form phrases of their own but function inside a Noun Phrase (NP), Verb Phrase (VP), Adjective Phrase (AdjP), Adverb Phrase (AdvP), or Preposition Phrase (PP).

In Section 1, the structure of phrases is studied and in Section 2, the structure for a full sentence and its phrases is discussed. The head of a phrase is important, but often this is intuitively understood. Phrases are very often coordinated by means of *and* or *or* and a structure for this is given in Section 3. In Section 4, more precise rules are given on how to identify phrases, and in Section 5 on how to construct trees.

1.   The phrase

1.1   The Noun Phrase (NP)

An NP such as *the nice unicorn* is built around a noun, namely, *unicorn*. This noun is called the head of the NP. In addition to the head, NPs can contain determiners (e.g. *the*) and adjectives (*nice*) as well as other elements. A tree structure for an NP is given in (1). The lines, called 'branches', indicate how the phrase is divided up, and branches come together in 'nodes':

1.

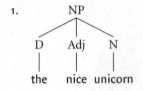

A different structure for (1) looks like (2):

2.

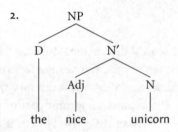

A structure such as (2) expresses the relationships more accurately than (1). In (1), it is unclear whether *the* specifies the adjective or the noun; in (2), *the* specifies *nice unicorn*. A structure as in (1) with more than two branches is a flat structure since the hierarchies are not clear. In this book, I will mainly use structures such as (2).

There are a number of things to note. First, the top node (i.e. where the branches come together) is always a phrase, an NP in this case; the node right above the *unicorn* is N. Second, the node in between the NP and N is called N′ (pronounced N-bar). It is an intermediate node and some people call it NOM. There can be more than one intermediate node, as we'll see in (7) below. Third, note that *nice* in (2) is itself the head of an Adjective Phrase (see 1.3 as well) and we could indicate that as in (3):

3.

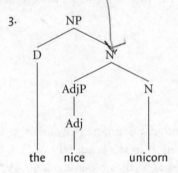

On occasion, it may be hard to find the head of an NP, or to identify the entire NP. For instance, the initial group of words in (4) is centered around a noun.

Which noun do you think is the head and how extended is the NP?

4.   The unpleasant unicorn from Malacandra loves dogfood.

The right answer is that *unicorn* is the head because if you had to shorten the sentence, you might say *the unicorn loves dogfood*. Thus, *unpleasant* and *from Malacandra* add additional information. Another way to shorten the sentence is to use a pronoun, as in (5). This is called pronominalization, and indicates that the phrase is *the unpleasant unicorn from Malacandra*:

5.   It loves dogfood.

You can also find the entire phrase by examining which parts say something about the head, i.e. modify it. Thus, in (4), both *unpleasant* and *from Malacandra* have no other function in the sentence than to modify the head *unicorn*.

We could represent (4) as (6):

6.

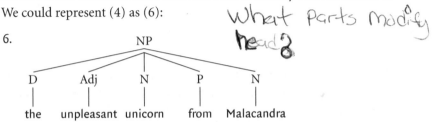

This structure indicates that the NP is composed of five words, but it does not say whether *from* is more connected to *Malacandra* or to *unicorn*. This is a flat structure since we don't see what goes with what. More hierarchical structures are given in (7ab):

7   a.

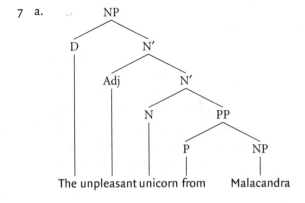

b.

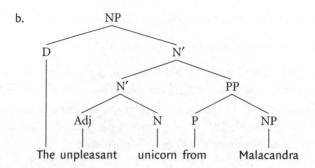

In (7a), *from Malacandra* goes together with *unicorn*. In a structure, this close connection is expressed by having the line, i.e. 'branch', that goes upwards connect to the same point, i.e. 'node'. This means they are 'sisters' in the structure. In (7b), *unpleasant* and *unicorn* are put closer together, i.e. are sisters. Both structures are possible. The meaning difference between (7a) and (7b) is minimal, but this is not always the case as sentences such as (15) and (17) below show.

Note again that *unpleasant* is itself the head of a phrase and that I am not indicating that. In addition, I am representing *Malacandra* as an NP without an N head. Typically, pronouns and names such as *Jennifer, Edward, Malacandra* cannot have other elements modify/specify them and therefore they are seen as full phrases. The ultimate tree is not as important as understanding why you represent a tree in a particular way, as I have just tried to do for (7).

Some heads seem trickier than others. For instance, in *one of those pages*, the head is *one*, and in *a piece of paper*, *piece* is the head. Frequently, a Relative Clause, *who wore that ugly hat* in (8) is part of an NP, as shown by brackets, modifying the head *person*:

8.   [The person [who wore that ugly hat]] is the queen.

A structure for (8) will be given in Chapter 10. For now, just understand that it is part of the NP.

Structures such as (7) are called trees. As mentioned, the lines connecting parts of the trees are called branches, and the points where the branches come together are called nodes. The nodes are usually labeled, e.g. N, N', or NP. Remember that N' is an intermediate between the top NP and the N. Such intermediate nodes allow one to indicate which elements are grouped together and thus make trees less flat.

1.2 The Adjective Phrase (AdjP) and Adverb Phrase (AdvP)

AdjPs are built around adjectives, which indicate properties of nouns; AdvPs
are built around adverbs which indicate qualities of verbs, adverbs, and adjectives. Since adjectives and adverbs have this qualifying function, they themselves
are (optionally) accompanied by a degree marker such as *very*, *too*, *extremely*,
really. The latter are adverbs of a special kind: they always modify another
adverb or adjective and never modify a verb. They are comparable to the
determiner in the NP, and more like grammatical than lexical categories. They
do not expand into an AdvP of their own.

An example of an Adjective Phrase is given in (9a) and of an Adverb Phrase in
(9b). The (D)Adv indicates a degree adverb. From now on, just Adv will be used:

9. a.   b.

In (9a), the head of the AdjP is the adjective *nice*, but this head is modified by a
degree adverb *so*; in (9b), the adverb *quickly* expands into a phrase and is
modified by the degree adverb *very* that does not form a phrase of its own.
That's why I choose not to make *very* the head of an AdvP.

An AdjP can be pronominalized, as in (10), but pronominalizing an AdvP,
as in (11), sounds awkward:

10. I was happy and **so** was she.

11. He behaved nicely, and she behaved **so/thus**.

1.3 The Verb Phrase (VP)

As was seen in Chapter 2, a VP is built around a verb, which can indicate an
action, as in (12a), a state, as in (12b), or a sensation, as in (12c). Verbs can be
in the present or past tense (they are past in (12abc)). Some VPs include other
obligatory material, i.e. words or phrases that cannot easily be left out, such as
the NP in (12a), the PP in (12b), and the AdjP in (12c). These obligatory parts
will be discussed in the next chapters:

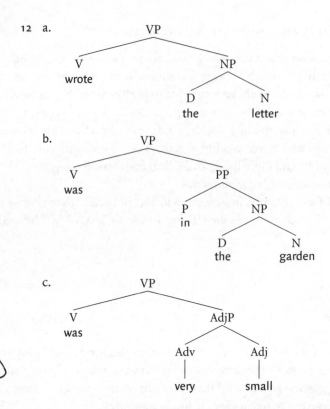

12 a. (VP tree: V "wrote", NP → D "the", N "letter")

b. (VP tree: V "was", PP → P "in", NP → D "the", N "garden")

c. (VP tree: V "was", AdjP → Adv "very", Adj "small")

The VP can also include optional material that explains when, where, why, and how the action or state that the verb describes took place. These optional elements function as adverbials and will be discussed in Chapter 5.

As in the case of the NP, a VP can be pronominalized. An example is given in (13), where the (bolded) VP *washed the dishes* is replaced by *do so*. Some linguists called these pro-VPs or pro-forms, since they do not stand for nouns. It is up to you whether you call them pronoun or pro-form:

13. John **washed the dishes** and Maija **did so** as well.

1.4 The Prepositional Phrase (PP)

A PP is built around a preposition. As mentioned in the previous chapter, prepositions indicate relations in space and time. PPs include a P and an NP, as in (14):

14.

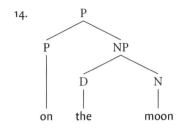

PPs can be replaced (pronominalized) by *then, there,* etc, which I have called adverbs above.

In this section, it is necessary to jump ahead to Chapters 4, 5, 9 and 10 where functions are discussed. Up to now, we have looked at the names of categories and phrases, e.g. N and NP. Depending on where phrases are situated in the tree, they play a particular function, such as subject and object. Functions will not be put in the tree structure because it should be clear from the tree.

With respect to PPs, it is not always easy to determine what the role is they play and their function in a sentence is manifold, as we'll see in Chapter 5. For instance, in the ambiguous (15), an often used sentence, does the PP function inside the NP, or are the NP and PP independent of one another?

15.   She saw the man with glasses.

The answer to both questions is 'yes' because the sentence is ambiguous. In the one case, the PP *with glasses* modifies the *man* and functions inside the NP *the man with glasses*; in the other case, the PP is independent of the NP since it modifies the VP and specifies how the seeing was done. The structure for the former reading is as in (16a) and for the latter reading as in (16b):

16   a.
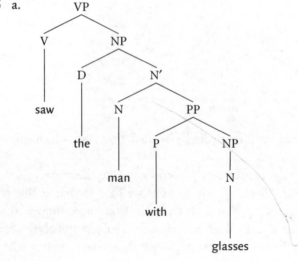

b.
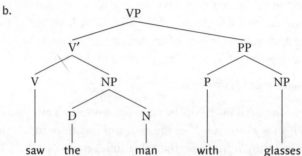

Thus, a particular tree structure disambiguates the sentence. In (16a), the PP *with glasses* is right next to the N *man* (i.e. PP is sister to N) and therefore modifies *man*; in (16b), the same PP is right next to the V′ *saw the man* (i.e. PP is sister to V′) and hence says something on how the seeing of the man is done. For now, don't worry about (16b) too much. You may have noticed the use of V′ (pronounced V-bar) in (16b). A V′ (like the N′ in an NP) is an intermediate category in the VP. We will come back to this in Chapter 5.

Groucho Marx uses structural ambiguity a lot, as in (17) below. Consider how the PP *in my pajamas* in (17) is ambiguous, in at least two ways:

17.   I once shot an elephant in my pajamas. How he got in my pajamas I'll
      never know.

There is a funny interpretation, namely, that the elephant is wearing the pajamas of the speaker while being shot. This is represented by (18a) where the

PP is part of the NP. The straightforward interpretation is that the speaker shot an elephant while the speaker was wearing pajamas, represented by (18b). There is a third (again funny) interpretation I will not go into here:

18 a.

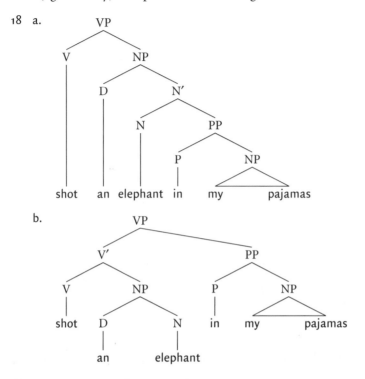

b.

Notice that I am being 'sloppy' with *my pajamas*. I represent that phrase by means of a 'coathanger', and am not indicating that the NP can be divided into a D and an N. It shows that in this particular tree, we are not really interested in the structure of *my pajamas*. However, I will try to avoid doing this in the remainder of the book.

As explained in Chapter 1, structural ambiguity is different from lexical ambiguity. With lexical ambiguity, a word has two meanings, e.g. *case* in Chapter 1. Another instance is (19), a well-known joke, where the preposition *outside* is lexically ambiguous. *Outside* and *inside* look like each other's opposites in expressing a location, but in fact *outside* has an additional meaning, namely 'in addition to; except for':

19. Outside of a dog, a book is a man's best friend; inside it's too hard to read.

2.   Phrases in the sentence

Having provided a tree structure for all of the phrases whose heads are lexical categories, I will now show how to combine these into a sentence. The basic structure for a sentence (i.e. S) is shown in (20):

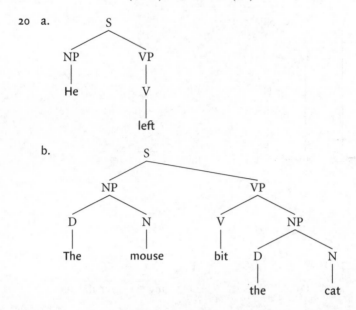

Thus, the initial element in the sentence is generally an NP (as we'll see in the next chapter, the function of this NP is subject). The NP is a daughter of the sentence S (i.e. immediately below S and connected by a tree branch). The rest of the sentence is the VP which can be more complex (as seen in (12), (16), and (18) above) as can the NP (as seen in (7)).

In the previous chapter, pronouns such as *he* in (20a) are argued to be both somewhat grammatical and somewhat lexical. They don't have much meaning but are the heads of phrases. In terms of a tree structure, pronouns are seen as representing the entire NP, and not as an N inside an NP. The main reason is that they cannot be modified by an adjective or article (**nice he; *the he*).

The relationships that are relevant in a tree are sister and daughter/mother. In (20ab), the NP and VP are sisters to each other and daughters of S. Sisters have a close relationship. Thus, in (16a), the relationship between the V *saw* and the NP *the man with glasses* is a direct one since they are sisters, but the relationship between *glasses* and the V *saw* is an indirect one.

As we'll see in the next chapter, each phrase has a function to play in the sentence. These functions can be read off the tree. For instance, in (20ab), the NP is the subject and the VP is the predicate; in (12a), the verb *wrote* is the head of the VP and its sister, the NP *the letter*, is the object.

3. Coordination of phrases

Phrases and categories can be coordinated, as long as they are the same kind. For instance, in (21), two pronouns are coordinated, in (22), two prepositions are, and in (23), two VPs are:

21. [She] and [I] got together.
22. The dog went [under] and [over] the fence.
23. I [read books] and [listened to music].

When the elements that are coordinated are not the same, e.g. an NP and a PP in (24), the sentence becomes ungrammatical:

24. *I read [a book] and [to Janet].

Coordination can be used to recognize phrases and categories. If you know one phrase or category, then the other will be the same phrase or category.

The structure for coordinate constructions is controversial. A number of linguists argue that the relationship between the coordinated phrases is completely equal and hence that a structure as in (26a) is appropriate. Others feel that the first phrase is somewhat more important and use (26b). Note that I have not labeled the node above *and* in (26b) since its name is controversial:

25. Books and magazines sell easily.
26. a.

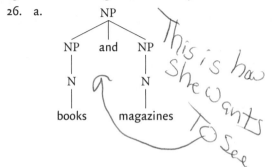

b.

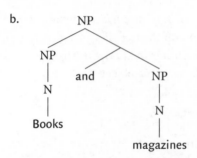

Arguments can be found for either structure. For ease of representation, I'll use (26a), but feel free to use (26b). We can usually switch around the NPs in (25) and this seems to be an argument in favor of (26a) since both NPs have the same status. However, when we move part of the *books and magazines*, for instance, because the second NP is a very long one, as in (27), *and* remains with the second NP and this speaks in favor of (19b) since *and magazines discussing political issues* is a unit (indicated by brackets in (27), but *books and* is not:

27.   I read books yesterday [and magazines discussing political issues].

In Chapter 7, we'll look at coordinating sentences, the basic question about which structure to pick is relevant there too.

Quite apart from having to choose one over the other, there is the added problem that we haven't seen an NP with another NP as daughter. This structure implies that there is one NP made up of two others. There are other such examples, namely appositive NPs, such as (28), from the *Preamble to the US Constitution*:

28.   We, the people of the United States, ... do ordain and establish ...

In (28), the second NP can replace the first, or could be rephased by a relative clause, as in (29). The structure could be as in (30), close to that of the relative clause in (29), as we'll see in Chapter 10:

29.   We, who are the people of the United States, ...

30.

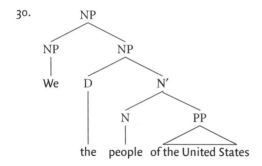

Two-part coordinators were mentioned in the previous chapter, e.g. *both Mary and John*; I will not provide a structure for these.

4. Finding phrases

A phrase is a group of words forming a unit and united around a head, e.g. a noun or a verb. Since phrases are syntactic units, a number of rules apply to them. Some of these have been discussed above, namely pronominalization and coordination. Three additional ones can be added. For instance, in (31), *to the store* is a phrase for the five reasons given in Table 3.1:

31. She ran to the store.

Table 3.1. Finding a phrase

a.	it can be pronominalized: *She ran there*;
b.	it can be coordinated with a phrase of the same kind: *She ran to the bookstore and to the library*;
c.	it can be deleted: *She ran*;
d.	it can be replaced by a *wh*-element: *Where did she run?*
e.	it can be moved: *To the store she ran.*

To the store is a PP because a Preposition, namely *to*, is the head.

All phrases can be pronominalized and coordinated. However, not all phrases can be deleted. The initial NP is very important, and in English, sentences are ungrammatical without it. Thus, changing (31) into (32) produces an ungrammatical sentence unless used in a very lively narrative:

32. *Ran to the store.

In Chapters 4 and 5, we will discuss what kinds of phrases can be deleted and what kinds cannot. Not all phrases can be replaced by a *wh*-element either: VPs cannot. When we question the sentence, we do so by moving the (auxiliary) verb, as in (33):

33. Will she run to the store?

The ability to move depends on the function the element plays in the sentence: optional/deletable elements can be moved more easily than obligatory ones. This is shown in (34) and (35); in (34), the optional *to the store* is moved with a grammatical result, but in (35), when the non-optional *the woman* is moved the result is an ungrammatical sentence:

34. To the store she ran.
35. *Ran to the store the woman.

5. Building trees

One can build trees from top to bottom or from bottom to top. Experiment with this a little. Let's do the phrase *the boy with a red hat* using both ways. Either way, we first need to decide what the head is. We'll argue it is *boy* (e.g. because we pronominalize the phrase with *he* not *it*). This means the phrase is an NP. Starting from the top, let's put down the NP first. If there is a determiner, the first branch to the left will always be to D, so D is the daughter of NP:

36.

Now, we have to be careful not to make the next branch go to N because then there won't be space for both the N *boy* and the PP *with the red hat*. Instead, we'll put down an N′ which can be expanded:

37.

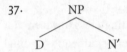

Now, the branches coming down from N′ need to be put in, as in (38):

38.

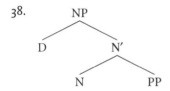

After this, finishing the tree is easy. We'll draw branches from PP to P and NP, and then have to start all over again with the NP. After the NP is finished, we must connect the words with lines to the categories underneath. The result will be as in (39):

39.

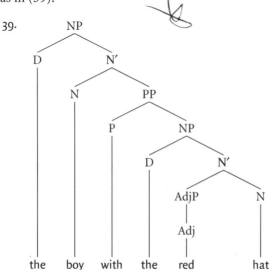

We could also have put the words closer to their categories, as I have done in most of the book, e.g. (16a) and (20) above.

Starting from the bottom, it is handiest to put the category of each word on top of it, as in (40):

40. D   N   P   D   Adj   N

    the   boy   with the   red   hat

Then, we need to find what goes with what. In this case, *red* and *hat* combine, so we'll draw branches to connect them:

41.

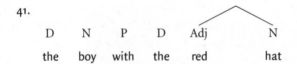

D	N	P	D	Adj	N
the	boy	with	the	red	hat

Then, D has to be combined with it and then P, with the result of (42):

42.

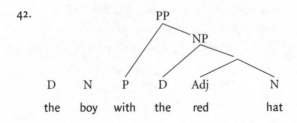

D	N	P	D	Adj	N
the	boy	with	the	red	hat

Now, the PP has to be connected to *boy* since it modifies it, and then D has to, and the result will be the same as that from the top to bottom process in (39). We'll need to make sure all nodes have labels, e.g. we need to put in the N′.

6. Conclusion

In this chapter, phrases and their tree structure are introduced. A lexical category such as a noun typically has other elements around it that modify it. This group of words and the head form a phrase. All lexical categories head phrases and each of these is discussed. Phrases are combined into sentences (or S), as in (20) above. A structure for phrases that are coordinated is also given.

The key terms in this chapter are **phrases (NP, VP, AdjP, AdvP and PP); S; flat as opposed to non-flat/hierarchical structures; ambiguity; pronominalization; and coordination.**

Exercises:

A. Identify the phrases in (43) to (46). Find the NP and VP that are sisters to each other, as well as the phrases inside the VP:

43. Tom submits his tax-return on time every year.

44. Kim's painting made Max extremely unhappy.

45. Everyone seemed extraordinarily self-confident at the time.

46. He remained an agnostic all his life.

B. Draw the tree structure in (47) to (49):

47. They planted a dogwood tree near the park.

48. The trees in the park are unhappy.

49. The man with the monstrously ugly umbrella left the house.

C. What do trees express?

D. Sentence (50) is ambiguous. Draw two trees indicating the ambiguity by means of a different structure. Which element is sister to which one?

50. I hit the Martian with a telescope.

E. Indicate the structure of (51) by means of a tree structure. Is (51) ambiguous? If so, explain how:

51. They like a house with a porch with rocking chairs.

F. Draw a structure for (52) and (53):

52. Tom and Jerry make good ice cream.

53. They washed dishes and cleaned the sink.

G. **Optional.** Give some reasons justifying your choice of some of the phrases in A.

Class discussion

H. In Chapter 1, Section 1.2, two instances of structural ambiguity are given. Can you explain the ambiguity in terms of structure?

I. Discuss the structure of *one of these, a piece of chalk,* and *all those arguments.*

Keys to the Exercises

A. – In (43), [Tom] is an NP and [submits his tax-return on time every year] is a VP; [his tax-return] is an NP; [on time] is a PP and [every year] is an NP.

- In (44), [Kim's painting] is an NP and [made Max extremely unhappy] is a VP; [Kim] is another NP; [Max] an NP; and [extremely unhappy] an AdjP.
- In (45), [Everyone] is an NP; [seemed extraordinarily self-confident at the time] a VP; [extraordinarily self-confident] an AdjP; and [at the time] a PP.
- In (46), [He] is an NP; [remained an agnostic all his life] is a VP; [an agnostic] an NP and [all his life] an NP.

B.   The tree for (47) is:

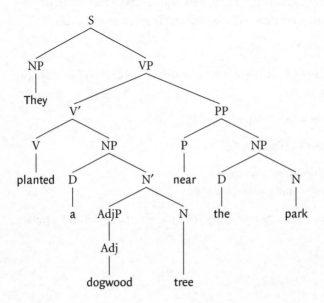

The tree for (48) is:

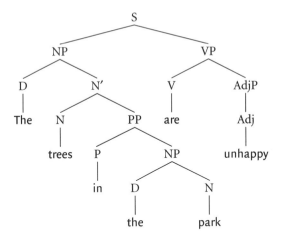

The tree for (49) is:

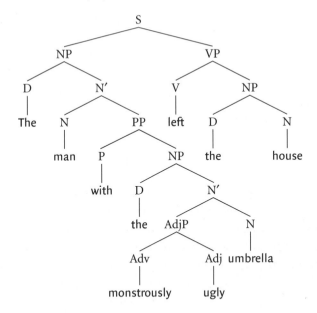

C. Trees indicate what goes with what, e.g. which phrases modify which head.

D. In the first tree, the Martian has a telescope; in the second tree, the 'she' has a telescope:

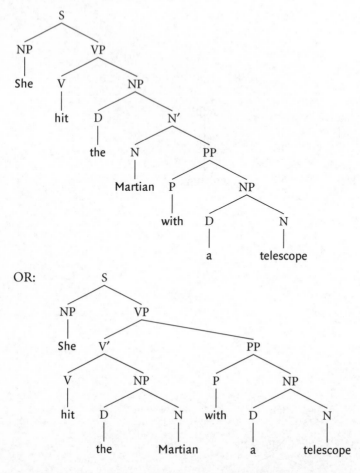

OR:

E. If the structure for (51) is the one drawn in (a), they like a house with both
    a porch and with rocking chairs and the rocking chairs can be anywhere in
    the house. If it is drawn as in (b), they like a house with a porch that has
    rocking chairs and the rocking chairs have to be on the porch. Tree (b)
    makes a lot more 'sense' than (a). Do you agree?

a.

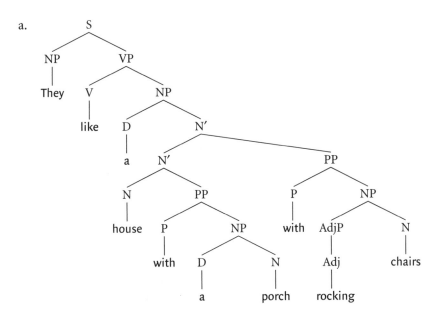

b.

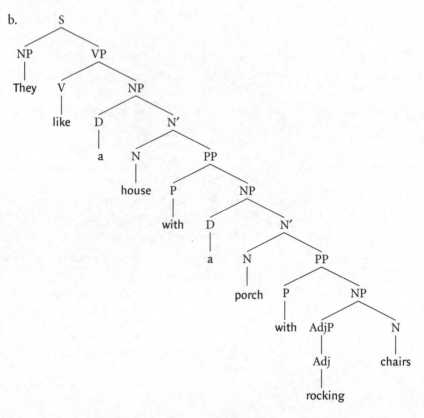

F.   The structures for (52) and (53) are as follows:

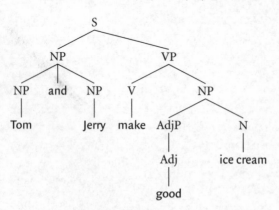

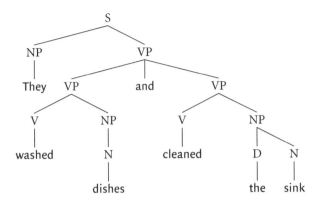

G. In (43), *Tom* is an NP because it can be pronominalized, i.e. replaced by *he*;
it can be coordinated with another NP as in *Tom and his accountant submit
the forms on time*. It cannot be deleted or moved because it is the subject as
we will see in Chapter 4. It can be questioned as in *Who submits the forms
on time?*

   Submits his tax-return on time every year is a VP since it can be pronominalized, i.e. replaced by *do so* as in *Tom submits his tax-return on time every
year and Jeremy does so too*. It can also be coordinated with another VP as in
*Tom submits his tax-return on time every year but neglects to renew his car
insurance*.

   His tax-return is an NP since it can be replaced by *it*, can be coordinated
as in *Tom submits his tax-return and insurance claims on time every year*, and
moved as in *It is his tax-return that Tom submits on time every year*.

   And so on...

Special topic: Negative Concord

Unlike most of the special topics, Negative Concord does not supplement the
material covered in the above chapter, but is an often debated issue.

   The prescriptive rule is as follows: "Two negatives in one sentence make the
sentence positive", or as Swan (1980:182) puts it "[i]n standard English,
nobody, nothing, never etc are themselves enough to make the sentence negative,
and *not* is unnecessary".

   We use certain types of multiple negatives in our utterances all the time, e.g.
in (54) and (55b). In (54), the sentence expresses negation since the *no* is

outside and independent of the *I don't want to go*. In this sentence, the negatives do not cancel each other out, since the negatives are independent of each other, and the sentence is prescriptively correct. In (55b), an answer to (55a), *nothing* is negated and the sentence could be paraphrased as (56). In this sentence, the negatives cancel each other out:

54. No, I don't want to go.
55. a: I paid nothing for that.
    b: Five dollars is not nothing.
56. Five dollars is quite something.

Since (54) and (55) follow the rule, they are not objected to by prescriptive grammarians.

A sentence such as (57), however, is said to be incorrect if it means the same as (58) or (59):

57. They don't have no problems.
58. They don't have problems.
59. They don't have any problems.

Although two negatives are supposed to make a positive, most speakers understand (57) as a negative. This construction is referred to as Negative Concord, i.e. the two negatives work together to emphasize the negation rather than cancel each other out. Sentences such as (57) occur very frequently in spoken, informal English. However, the prescriptive rule is so well known that people often deliberately break it for impact. That may have been the reason a double negative is used in (60), a protest sign at the time that a student code of conduct was being considered at the University of Michigan in Ann Arbor:

60.

Another reason may be that the negation on *do* is perhaps felt as too weak in English and that's the reason behind adding another negative. In earlier English, as discussed in Chapter 1, multiple negation was very common, perhaps because *not* was not a contracted form yet.

Review Chapters 1–3

The first chapter shows that we know quite a bit about language intuitively without formal training and the second and third chapters make some of this knowledge explicit. Chapter 2 lists the lexical and grammatical categories we make use of, and Chapter 3 shows how sentences can be divided into phrases, each of which is centered around a noun, verb, adjective, adverb, or preposition.

Exercises relevant to these chapters

A. List the categories in (1), both lexical and grammatical. Give two reasons why *painted* is a verb:

    1. Zoya painted the chairs in the rain.

    Provide the phrase structure or tree for (1).

B. Is (1) ambiguous? Depending on your answer, explain why or why not.

C. Please list the lexical and grammatical categories in (2) and (3). Draw a tree for (2):

    2. The pig from Mars ate his food.
    3. Do not go gentle into that good night,
        Old age should burn and rave at close of day; ...

D. Draw trees for the phrases in (4) and (5) and the sentences in (6) and (7) and discuss your findings:

    4. That careless driver on the street.
    5. noticed a hopeless mess.
    6. Vincent and his brother wrote many letters.
    7. We suggested those solutions quickly.

Class discussion

E.   Please comment on 'You look real nice'. When would you say this; when might you say something else.

F.   Explain the difference between linguistic and non-linguistic knowledge.

Keys to the Exercises

A.   Zoya: N

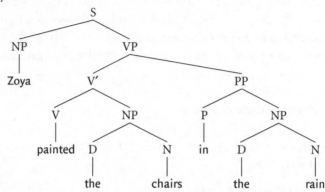

painted: V
the: D
chairs: N
in: P
the: D
rain: N

Painted is a verb because it shows past tense (morphological) and indicates an action (semantic).

B.   No, it is not since *in the rain* is independent of *chairs*; it says something about where Zoya painted them.

C. The: D

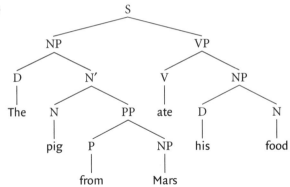

pig: N
from: P
Mars: N
ate: V
his: D
food: N

In (3): Do (AUX) not (Adv) go (V) gentle (Adj) into (P) that (D) good (Adj) night (N), Old (Adj) age (N) should (AUX) burn (V) and (C) rave (V) at (P) close (N) of (P) day (N).

D.

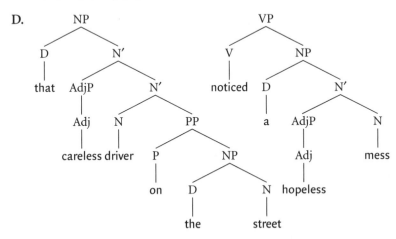

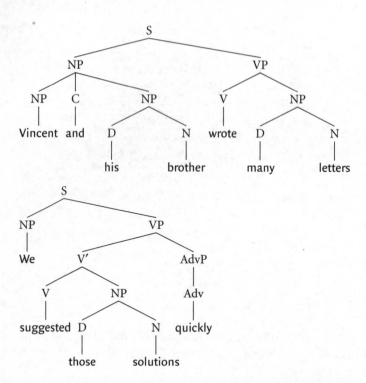

4 Functions in the sentence

In Chapter 3, groups of words that go together were called phrases and divided into NP, VP, AdjP, AdvP, and PP. Phrases (and pronouns since they replace phrases) have functions in the sentence, e.g. subject, direct object, indirect object, and subject and object predicate. The name, label, or realization of the function (e.g. NP) and the function itself (e.g. subject) should be kept separate. As mentioned, we will not be putting functions in the tree structures since (most of) the functions follow from the tree structure, or to put it differently, certain functions such as subject and direct object occupy specific positions in the tree (daughter of S and sister of V respectively), and to label them would be redundant.

The four basic functions are subject, predicate, complement, and adverbial (see next chapter for adverbials). A subject and predicate are needed in every sentence. Certain verbs need complements as well. Complements come in different varieties; the ones dealt with in this chapter are direct object, indirect object, subject predicate, and object predicate. Some people equate object and complement, but technically complement is a broader category than object.

1. The different functions and how they are realized

1.1 Subject and Predicate

Every complete sentence has a subject and a predicate. The subject is usually realized by an NP (sometimes by a clause, see Chapter 7), and the predicate is realized by a VP. In (1), *the moon* is the subject and *has risen in the sky* is the predicate. The predicate says something about the subject:

1. The moon has risen in the sky.

The table below lists three diagnostics for determining what the subject is. Try to apply these to (1):

Table 4.1. Subject tests (subject is in italics; verb is in bold)

a.	Inversion in *Yes/No* questions
	The pig from Malacandra **will** want to eat soon →
	Will *the pig from Malacandra* want to eat soon?
b.	Agreement with the Verb/AUX
	The pfiftrigg **is** nice → *The pfiftriggs* **are** nice.
c.	Tag questions
	The hross **is** nice, **isn't** *he*?

Applying the first test to (1), as in (2), shows that *the moon* is the subject since it changes places with *has*. To use the second test, we need to change the subject and see if that changes the verb as well, indicating there is agreement. In (3), the subject is pluralized and the verb becomes plural as well (i.e. loses the third person singular ending). This shows *the moon* in (1) is indeed the subject. The sentence is a bit strange since there is only one moon in the real world. However, if we were on Jupiter, (3) would be appropriate. Hence, the strangeness is not caused by the grammar, but by our knowledge of the world:

2. Has the moon just risen in the sky?
3. The moons have just risen in the sky.

The third test involves adding a tag question and seeing what the pronoun in the tag replaces. In (4), the *it* in the tag refers to *the moon* and not to *the sky* and that's why the former is the subject:

4. The moon has just risen in the sky, hasn't it?

Having discussed three criteria for identifying subjects, I turn to a kind of subject that, at first, does not look like a subject, namely, *there* in (5):

5. There are five unicorns in the parking lot.

If we apply the above tests to (5), *there* and *five unicorns* each pass some, but not all, of the tests for subject. For instance, in a question *there* and *are* switch places; the tag will be formed with *there* as in *aren't there*; but the agreement on the verb is determined by *five unicorns*. To account for this, we'll assume that both *there* and *five unicorns* function as the subject. *There* is called a dummy or pleonastic subject. It is used when no other subject occupies the position in the beginning of the sentence. A variant of (5) is (6), where *five unicorns* is in subject position and *there* is not needed:

6. Five unicorns are in the garden.

1.2 Direct and Indirect Object

A common function is the direct object, usually realized as an NP, as in (7) and (8) (see Chapter 7 for the use of a clause as direct object):

7. Harry Potter played [a game].
8. My owl read [the letter from Hogwarts].

Objects occur as sisters to the verb, as in (9), and can be passivized, as in (10):

9.

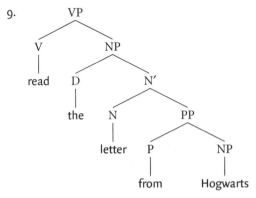

10. The letter from Hogwarts was read by my owl.

Passive sentences are variants of non-passive or active ones and come about by switching the subject and the object and by adding a form of *to be* as in (11b), the passive variant of (11a). The subject of the active sentence (11a) becomes optional in the passive, and if expressed is preceded by *by*:

11. a. I saw him.
     b. He was seen by me.

Passivization is a way to distinguish between objects (both direct and indirect) on the one hand and subject predicates, object predicates, and adverbials on the other, as we'll see in the next chapter.

The indirect object, which is always an NP, expresses the goal (*Santa* in (12)) or the beneficiary of the action (*Harry* in (13)):

12. I gave Santa a letter.
13. I made Harry some soup.

Indirect objects can be passivized as well, and in a sentence with both a direct and indirect object, it is the indirect object that becomes the subject. For instance, (14) is the passive counterpart of (12), and the indirect object *Santa* becomes the subject, not the direct object *a letter*.

14. Santa was given a letter by me.

Indirect objects can be preceded by the prepositions *to*, in the case of the goal, and *for*, in the case of a beneficiary, as in (15) and (16):

15. I gave a letter to Santa.
16. I made some soup for Harry.

When *to* and *for* are added the order of indirect and direct object switches, as you can see by comparing (12) with (15). Some grammarians call the PPs *to Santa* and *for Harry* indirect objects; others call them adverbials since they seem less important to the sentence, e.g. some can be left out, and they cannot become the subject of a passive sentence, as the unacceptable (17) shows:

17. *Santa was given a letter to.

1.3 Subject and Object Predicate

The subject predicate is usually realized as an AdjP. It makes a claim about the subject, as in (18), and can also be an NP, as in (19), or a PP, as in (20) (see Chapter 7 for the use of a clause as subject predicate):

18. He is pleasant.
19. He is a nice person.
20. He is in the garden.

The verb used in sentences with a subject predicate is usually either *be* or *become* or can be replaced by it. Thus, in the poem by Dylan Thomas, discussed in exercise F of Chapter 2, the adjective *gentle* is predicated of the unexpressed subject and the verb *go* could be replaced by *become*. Other verbs that typically occur with a subject predicate are *feel, look, grow, smell*, when used as in (21):

21. This silk feels nice; that problem looks hard; she grew tired; that smells nice.

As mentioned in the special topic to Chapter 2, many speakers overreact or panic when they produce an adjective right next to a verb, as in (21). The combination is correct since the adjective modifies a noun, and it need not be changed to an adverb and in many cases it can't be.

The verbs in (21) can be used in other ways too and that's why it is important to think about the entire sentence and not just to look at the verb. Thus, in (22), *feel* has a direct object, namely *his pulse*:

22. He felt his pulse.

In (18) and (21), the adjective says something about the subject, but an adjective can also say something about a (direct) object function and then functions as an object predicate. The object predicate is usually an adjective phrase, as in (23), but can also be an NP, as in (24), or a PP, as in (25):

23. She painted the house purple.
24. Jane considers *Pride and Prejudice* a classic.
25. She put the cup on the table.

Here too, it sometimes depends on your analysis whether you consider a phrase an object predicate or a direct object. For instance, *a good chairperson* in (26) can be a predicate to the direct object *him*, in which case *to be* can occur between them, as in (27), and *him* is the same person as *a good chairperson*. Alternatively, *him* can be an indirect object and *a good chairperson* a direct object, in which case *for* can precede *him*, as in (28), and *him* and *a good chairperson* are not the same person. Hence, the verb *find* is ambiguous:

26. They found him a good chairperson.
27. They found him to be a good chairperson.
28. They found for him a good chairperson.

The terms for the two functions discussed in this section are much debated. Some grammarians call them subject and object complements; others subject and object predicatives; yet others call them subject and object attributives. I have chosen subject and object predicate to show that their function is similar to that of the VP predicate. It is as if the AdjP is more important than the verb in these constructions. That is the reason the verb in (18) to (20) can be left out in many languages and, in English, no verb appears to link object and object predicate, even though *to be* can be included in (24), as (29) shows:

29. Jane considers *Pride and Prejudice* to be a classic.

In short, some of the major functions of phrases in the sentence are subject, predicate, direct and indirect object, subject predicate, and object predicate. There are special objects such as prepositional objects and objects of phrasal verbs. These will be dealt with in Chapter 5 together with the optional adverbial function.

2.   Verbs and functions

Verbs are distinguished depending on what objects or object predicates they select. Verbs that select objects are called transitive verbs and those that don't, as in (30) below, intransitive. If the verb selects one object, as in (8) above, it is (mono)transitive; if it selects two objects as in (12) and (13), it is ditransitive. Verbs that select a subject predicate, as in (18) and (21), are called copula verbs or linking verbs and those that have both an object and an object predicate, as in (23) to (25), are called complex transitive. In the next chapter, two more types of verbs will be discussed: prepositional and phrasal verbs. Since adverbials can always be added to any verb, they do not play a role in the classification of the verb. I will now provide examples of each kind of verb.

Examples of intransitives are *swim, walk, arrive, cough, sleep*, and *sneeze*:

30. He sneezed and sneezed.
31. He slept during the meeting.

As mentioned before, you need to look at the context before you can be completely sure of the classification. Thus, *walk* in *I walk the dog* is transitive, but in *I walked for hours* it is not. (In the next chapter, Section 5, I give some reasons why *during the meeting* in (31) is not an object).

Examples of (mono)transitives are *eat, read, see, hear, plant, write, compose, paint, love, hate, drink*, and *hit*, as in (32):

32. He hit the ball.

Give, tell, bake, cook, and *play* as in (33) are ditransitives:

33. I played him a tune.

If a verb selects a subject predicate, it is called a copula verb. A number of copula or linking verbs were given above, namely *be, become, go, feel, look, grow, seem, smell*. Complex transitives are verbs such as *consider, know, elect, keep, prove, deem, judge, reckon, make*, and *regard*. They have direct objects and object predicates as their complements. In Chapter 5, I'll summarize the classification of verbs in a table. Please notice (again) that many verbs belong to more than one category. For instance, *make* can be a transitive, as in *I made tea*, or a complex transitive, as in *She made them happy*, or a ditransitive, as in (16) above.

Distinctions such as transitive and intransitive are useful to explain when to use verb forms such as *lay/lie, set/sit*, and *fell/fall*. The first verb in the set is the transitive, as in (34), and the second is the intransitive, as in (35). An added problem with these lies in their past tense forms, which may be the same as the present for the other verb:

34. The chicken lays an egg every day; he laid a book on the table yesterday; I have laid the table like this for years.
35. I lie down regularly; I lay down yesterday; I have lain here for hours.

3. Trees

As I have mentioned before, the tree structure reflects what the function of each phrase is. Thus, the subject and the predicate are the daughters of S, and the objects and predicates are sisters to V. The adverbial elements, as we'll see in the next chapter, are not sisters to V, but the prepositional objects and objects to phrasal verbs are.

Intransitives may occupy the entire VP, as in (36):

36.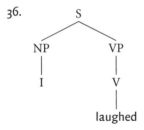

A structure for the (mono)transitive verb of (32) above is (37), and for the copula verb of (21) above, it is (38):

37.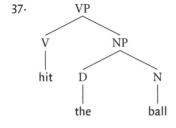

38.

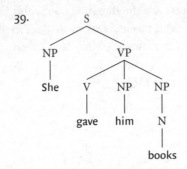

In general, we try to make trees show hierarchies, i.e. we seek to avoid triple branches in (39). However, to show that both the direct and indirect object in (39) are objects, I have drawn them as sisters to the V:

39.

There are ways of expressing this in a non-flat/hierarchical structure but they are complicated and still controversial. Hence, this book will use (39), noting the problem of the flatness.

The other verb where flatness is a problem is the complex transitive one in (23) to (25) above. Since the object and predicate in some way form a unit (unlike the direct and indirect object), I'll represent it as in (40), labeling the node above NP and AdjP a small clause (SC), i.e. a clause with the verb deleted:

40.

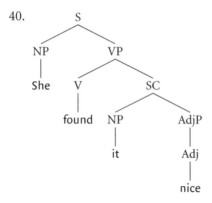

4. Light verbs (Optional)

This is an introductory grammar text, and hence not all kinds of verbs can be dealt with. To give an example of such a group, we'll look at light verbs, an interesting set of verbs in English that combines with nouns (and sometimes determiners and prepositions also). Examples are *have/take a look, give advice (on), make a decision (on), do a translation (of), do harm, give a hand, take a rest, make trouble (for)*. The verb and noun together have the meaning of a verb, e.g. *have/take a look* is similar to the verb *look*, *give advice* to the verb *advise*, and *make a decision* to the verb *decide*. With some, e.g. *do a translation*, the noun is still a real object and can be passivized, as in *That translation of Homer was done by a famous writer*; with some, e.g. *take a look*, the passive sounds strange, as in *A look was taken by me*. We won't draw trees for these or analyze them further.

5. Conclusion

In this chapter, I have discussed the major functions that phrases fulfill: subject, direct and indirect object, subject predicate, and object predicate. Another way of saying this is that a particular function is realized by a particular phrase. In Table 4.2, a schematic representation for the functions of NP, VP and AdjP is given. Apart from VP, which is always a predicate (and the other way round), there is no one-to-one relationship between a phrase and a function. In Chapter 5, PPs and AdvPs will be discussed:

Table 4.2. A schema of the functions of NPs, VPs, and AdjPs

Subject (*[the driver] laughed*)	<	>	Subject Predicate (*is [a student]*)
Direct Object (*see [the problem]*)	<	NP >	Object Predicate (*consider him [a fool]*)
Indirect Object (*give [the dog] food*) <		>	Adverbial (*left [today]*, see chap 5)
		VP =	Predicate (*He [saw the clock]*)
Subject Predicate (*is [nice]*)	<	AdjP >	Object Predicate (*consider him [foolish]*)

The classification of verbs is dependent on the kinds of objects and predicates they have. Thus, intransitives have no objects, (mono)transitives have one, and ditransitives have two objects. Copula verbs have a subject predicate and complex transitive verbs have an object and an object predicate. Tree structures are also provided for each of these verbs. Key terms are **functions (subject, direct and indirect object, subject predicate, and object predicate); classification of verbs (intransitive, (mono)transitive, ditransitive, copula, and complex transitive)**.

Exercises

A. How many functions have we discussed so far? Provide an example of each.

B. Identify the subjects in the text used in Chapter 2, repeated here:

> At last, we had begun filming. Should I say 'we'? I was living in the house and extremely curious about everything connected with the film. Fortunately, they let me hang around and even gave me a job. As an historian, I kept an eye on detail and did not allow the filmmakers to stray too far from the period of Louis Philippe. The project was to make an hour-long film about Houdin and it was decided to shoot the picture in Switzerland. This may have been a bad idea. It certainly mixed professional and domestic affairs.

C. Identify the functions of the phrases in the sentences below:

41. I gave him the saguaro.
42. They planted a dogwood.
43. The trees in the park are unhappy.

D. Identify the different kinds of complements (e.g. direct object, subject predicate) in (44) to (50). Give reasons:

44. They sold us their furniture.
45. Tom submits his tax-returns.

46. She seemed very happy.
47. He found it easy.
48. He took the early train.
49. The politician considered that argument invalid.
50. That sounds terrible.

E. Provide the labels of the main verbs in (44) to (50) (e.g. copula, ditransitive) and draw trees.

F. Find 4 intransitive verbs and 4 copula verbs (other than the ones discussed in the book). Also, please provide 4 sentences with a direct and 4 sentences with an indirect object.

G. List all the functions and names/labels of the phrases in (51) to (54):

51. I considered the book very helpful.
52. He baked Joan a cake.
53. The pig from Mars left.
54. The hard-working students seemed exhausted.

To what categories do the following words belong: *helpful, from, hard-working*?

H. Look at the first page of Mavis Gallant's short story "About Geneva" below:

> Granny was waiting at the door of the apartment. She looked small, lonely, and patient, and at the sight of her the children and their mother felt instantly guilty. Instead of driving straight home from the airport, they had stopped outside Nice for ice cream. They might have known how much those extra twenty minutes would mean to Granny. Colin, too young to know what he felt, or why, began instinctively to misbehave, dragging his feet, scratching the waxed parquet. Ursula bit her nails, taking refuge in a dream, while the children's mother, Granny's only daughter, felt compelled to cry in a high, cheery voice, "Well, Granny, here they are, safe and sound!"

What kinds of verbs are *wait, look, feel, drive*?

What is the function of *those extra twenty minutes, the waxed parquet, small, lonely, and patient*?

I. Identify the subjects in (55) to (58). Provide two reasons why in each case:

55. In the rain, it is sometimes hard to see.
56. Only one of these people is happy.

57.   The book Chomsky wrote when he was young was reissued last year.
58.   Were the Wizard of Oz and Catweazle preparing to go to Alabama?

Optional

J.   Sentence is (59) is quite complex. What kinds of verbs are *grow* and *look*?

59.   *Emma*, Vol 2, chap 1
      We must expect to see her grown thin, and looking very poorly.

Keys to the Exercises

A.   See Section 4, i.e. the conclusion.
B.   we, I, I, they, me, I, the filmmakers, the project, it, this, it. The reason that accusative *me* and *the filmmakers* are subjects will be clearer after chapter 8. For now, don't worry about these two.
C.   Su, Pred, IO, DO
     Su, Pred, DO
     Su, Pred, SuPred
D.   IO, DO
     DO
     SuPred
     DO, ObPred
     DO
     DO, ObPred
     SuPred
E.   ditransitive; transitive; copula; complex transitive; transitive; complex transitive; copula.

The tree for (44) is:

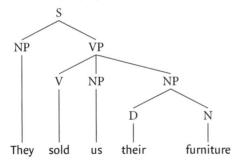

The tree for (45) is:

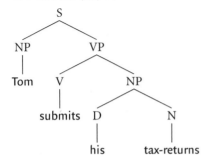

The tree for (46) is:

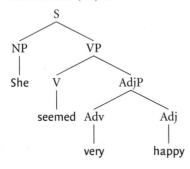

The tree for (47) is:

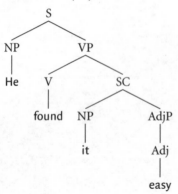

The tree for (48) is like the one for (45); the tree for (49) is similar to the one for (47); and the tree for (50) is similar to (46).

F.   Do in class.

G.   Su:NP, Pred:VP, DO:NP, ObjPred:AdjP
     Su:NP, Pred:VP, IO:NP, DO:NP
     Su:NP, Pred:VP
     Su:NP, Pred:VP, SuPred:AdjP

     Adj, P, Adj.

H.   *wait*: intransitive; *look*: copula; *feel*: copula; *drive*: intransitive (debatable). *those extra twenty minutes*: Su; *the waxed parquet*: DO; *small, lonely, and patient*: SuPred.

I.   In (55), *it*; in (56), *only two of those people*; in (57), *The book Chomsky wrote when he was young*; in (58), *the Wizard of Oz and Catweazle*. Not all criteria can be used in all cases:
     – In *Were the Wizard of Oz and Catweazle preparing to go to Alabama*, the subject and auxiliary have inverted since it is a question (hence no tag is possible), and without having to use inversion yourself, you can see what the subject is. The agreement on *were* is plural which fits if *the Wizard of Oz and Catweazle* are the subject. Notice that if you changed it to just the *Wizard*, the agreement becomes singular: *Was the Wizard preparing to go?*
     – You could use tag-questions in some (but not in questions):
       In the rain, it is sometimes hard to see, isn't it?

The book Chomsky wrote when he was young was reissued last year, wasn't it?

- In sentences that aren't already questions, such as (58), inversion would work as follows:
In the rain, is it sometimes hard to see?
Is only one of these people happy?
Was the book Chomsky wrote when he was young reissued last year?
- If you pluralized the subject, the verb would change as well (this is hard to do with *it* in (55) though):
Two of these people are happy.
The books Chomsky wrote when he was young were reissued last year.

J. It has two ambiguous verbs, namely *grow* and *look*, and the adjective *thin* is used as subject predicate to modify *her*. *Poorly* is used as subject predicate as well since it modifies the deleted subject of *looking*. So, even though it looks like an adverb, it is an adjective (the Oxford English Dictionary says that the use of *poorly* as an adjective is somewhat rare, but it is quite frequent in Jane Austen).

Special topic: Case

Reprinted with special permission of King Feature Syndicate.

Rule: "Subjects have **nominative** case. Direct and indirect objects have **accusative or objective** case. Prepositions also give **accusative or objective** case. Possessive nouns have **genitive** case".

In Modern English, these cases are only visible on pronouns. Thus, in (60), the subject *she* is nominative and *him* is accusative for reasons we'll go into in Chapter 8. *Me* is given case by the preposition *towards* and that case is also accusative. In (61), *you* and *me* have accusative case as well since they are case marked by the preposition *between*:

60.   She saw him come towards me.
61.   This is between you and me.

In (11) above, the case changes from nominative to accusative when a subject becomes a prepositional object, as happens in the passive. With full NPs, it is not obvious what the case is.

In coordinates, however, this rule is often broken in all stages of English. Thus, in (62), (63), and (64), the nominative *I* is used rather than the accusative *me*, and in (65), the accusative *thee* (this is a special form, no longer used) is used rather than the nominative *thou* (again no longer in use), expected since *the Diuell and thee* are the subject:

62.   Shakespeare, *Merchant of Venice* III, 2, 321
      all debts are cleared between you and I.
63.   If you are sick and tired of the way it's been going, ..., you give Al Gore and I
      a chance to bring America back. (Clinton, as reported in NYT 23 July 1992).
64.   In his speech, Mr. Giuliani said that one of the main differences between he
      and Mrs. Clinton was that "I'm in favor of reducing your taxes ..." (NYT, 8
      April 2000).
65.   Shakespeare 1 *Henry IV* I, 2, 126
      How agrees the Diuell and thee about thy soule?

Notice that in (65), the agreement on the verb is singular as well even though the subject is the plural *the Diuell and thee.*

With *wh*-questions, the case rule is also often broken. Thus, in (66), *whom* would sound very artificial even though, as the accusative or objective form, it is the correct form, as is evident from the cartoon below:

66.   Who did I meet?

BEETLE BAILEY by Mort Walker

Reprinted with special permission of King Feature Syndicate.

Before 1600 or so, in sentences with the copula verb *to be*, both subject and subject predicate have nominative case. Nowadays, this sounds overly formal.

The genitive case is used in phrases such as (67) and (68). If the word does not end in *s*, an apostrophe and *s* are added, as in (67), but if it ends in an *s*, as in (68), either an apostrophe and *s* or just an apostrophe is added. Many people consider the ending in (68) pedantic and hence it often disappears altogether:

67.   Shakespeare's works
68.   Employees'(s) cafeteria

5 More functions: of prepositions and particles

This chapter deals with adverbials, i.e. the optional elements in the sentences that provide background information on when, where, why, and how the event described by the verb and its objects takes place. It is important to be aware that adverbials are not always realized as AdvPs, but can also be realized as PPs (or as clauses, see Chapter 8). In a tree, phrases functioning as adverbials are sisters to V'.

Prepositional objects are also discussed since they look like adverbials, but can be shown not to be. Objects to phrasal verbs are regular direct objects. They are discussed here rather than in Chapter 4 because they are easily confused with prepositional objects and include a preposition-like element called a particle. Finally, two other kinds of verbs are discussed involving particles and prepositions: the intransitive phrasal verb and the phrasal prepositional verb.

The main point of this chapter is to learn to distinguish between adverbials and objects. I'll provide some tests for this.

1. Adverbials

When adverbials modify verbs, they express when, where, how, and why the action takes place. So, they give background information on time, place, manner, and cause of the event. In the tree structure, we make a distinction between direct and indirect objects, subject predicates, and object predicates on the one hand (all referred to as complements) and adverbials on the other: objects, subject predicates, and object predicates are closer to the verb than adverbials. Even if in the tree only the phrases have labels, and their functions are not indicated, you should be able to tell from the tree which phrase is the object and which is the adverbial in (1):

1.

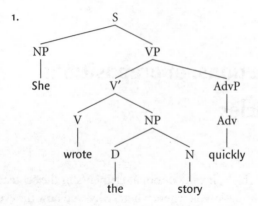

In (1), the NP *the story* is sister to the V *wrote* and is therefore the object; *quickly* is sister to the intermediate V' *wrote the story*, and therefore modifies that. *Quickly* tells you how the story was written and is therefore an adverbial. Since the V' that represents *wrote the story* is intermediate inside the VP, we call it a V' ('V-bar').

When you draw the tree, perhaps look back to Chapter 3 (Section 5) and remember possible ambiguities, e.g. in (16) of Chapter 3. I'll show how to construct the one in (1) quickly (from top to bottom). First, you start with S, the daughters of which are always NP and VP. The NP happens to be a pronoun, so nothing else needs to be done. The VP consists of a V *wrote*, an object *the story*, and an adverbial *quickly*. Be careful not to make the first branch (i.e. to the left) into a V because then you won't have space for all three. Instead, use the V', and then think what should be closest to the V, and fit them in:

2.

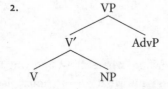

There is a difference between a VP-adverbial (e.g. *quickly* in (1)) and a sentence adverbial (e.g. *fortunately, actually, indeed, of course*). Sentence adverbials (or S-adverbials) do not modify the action of the VP but express the views and the mood of the speaker. Trees for a sentence-initial and sentence-final S-adverbial are given in (3). Duplicating the S intends to show that the adverbial is really outside the core sentence, which is often indicated by means of a comma:

3. a.

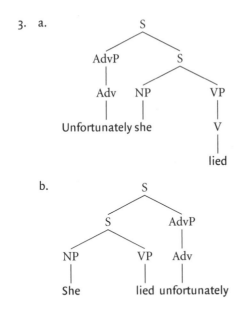

b.

I discuss *hopefully* in Chapter 2 (see special topics): for most speakers of English, *hopefully* is both a VP-adverbial and an S-adverbial. The same is true for adverbs such as *happily* in (4). There are two interpretations. One is where painting the pictures was a happy event, in which case, *happily* is a VP-adverbial modifying *painted those pictures*, and the comma is less appropriate. A second interpretation is where the speaker expresses an opinion about the entire sentence (perhaps because the pictures turned out to be good):

4. Happily, I painted those pictures.

The same ambiguity exists for adverbs such as *wisely* and *clearly*.

PPs that function as adverbials are typically VP-adverbials. They often provide background information regarding place, as in (5), and time, as in (6):

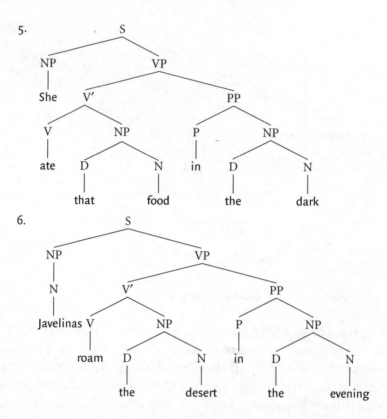

A sentence can have many adverbials (depending on the speaker's or hearer's patience). For instance, in (7), the speaker's feelings (*unfortunately*), the time (*that morning*), and place (*to work*) of driving the car are given, as well as the reason for this action (*the bus had broken down*) and the way in which the action occurred (*without glasses*):

7.   Unfortunately, he drove the car [to work] [that morning] [without his glasses] [because the bus had broken down].

It is possible to add more adverbials to this sentence, e.g. *quickly* or *recklessly*.

As can be seen in (7), adverbials are not only realized as AdvPs such as *quickly*, but also as NPs (*that morning*), PPs (*to work* and *without his glasses*), and clauses (*because the bus had broken down*, see Chapter 7). This means NPs function not only as subjects, indirect and direct objects, subject predicates and object predicates (see previous chapter), but also as adverbials. AdvPs on the other hand only function as adverbials. PPs function mainly as adverbials and subject predicates but, as we'll see in the next section, they also function as objects to certain verbs, namely prepositional ones (and, as we saw in Chapter 3 and will see in more detail in Chapter 9, they can also be modifiers inside a phrase).

2. Prepositional verbs

Prepositional verbs are verbs such as *abide by* in (8), *refer to* in (9), *glance at, lean against, add to, allow for, approve of, care for, insist on, resort to, apply for, account for, reply to, absolve from, long for, yearn for, argue about*, and *defer to* in which the P with the NP functions as an object:

8. They abided by the contract.
9. He referred to that article.

These verbs require a PP, i.e. (10) and (11) are ungrammatical, and that's why the PP is considered an object rather than an adverbial. *The contract* in (8) and *that article* in (9) can also be passivized, as in (12) and (13), and this test shows that they are real objects, as shown in (14), where the PP is sister to V:

10. *He abides.
11. *He refers all the time.
12. The contract was abided by.
13. That article wasn't referred to by him.
14.

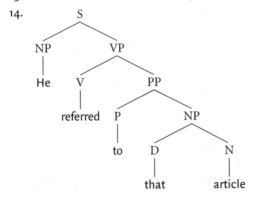

Native speakers of English know that verbs such as *refer* are combined with a certain preposition. Non native speakers must learn the meanings of these verbs or look them up in a dictionary, e.g. *refer with, refer about, refer at* are not possible.

3.   Phrasal verbs

Phrasal verbs must be distinguished from prepositional verbs and from verbs with an adverbial. Like prepositional verbs, they are listed separately in a dictionary since their combinations are somewhat idiosyncratic. Examples of phrasal verbs are *call up, bring up, cover up, take away, turn in, put down, take off, put on, switch on/off, hand in, make out* (as in 'decipher'). Some example sentences are given in (15) to (19):

15.   They called up the president.
16.   They covered up the scandal.
17.   Helen turned in her homework.
18.   She put down the nasty people.
19.   She switched on the light.

The prepositions *up, in, down,* and *on* accompanying these verbs have become particles rather than prepositions or adverbs since they no longer always express place or direction. The structure of a sentence such as (15) is therefore one of a verb with a particle, as in (20):

20.

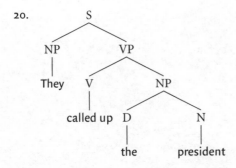

Thus, in (20), for the sake of convenience, the verb and particle are placed in V together, whereas the object is a separate NP.

One of the easy (but not so well understood) criteria for determining if a verb is phrasal is whether the (pronominalized) object can be put between the verb and the particle, as in (21) to (23):

21.   They called him up.
22.   They covered it up.
23.   She turned it in with many mistakes.
24.   She put them down.
25.   She switched it on.

This is not possible with prepositional verbs, as the ungrammatical (26) shows:

26. *They abided it by.

The basic distinction, clear from (20), is that the V and particle form a unit and that the object is an NP, not a PP. This is so because (a) a pause can occur between the verb–particle complex and the NP object, as in (27), but not between the V and the unit which is not a phrase as in (28); (b) the NP objects can be coordinated, as in (29), but the particle and NP cannot, as (30) shows; and (c) moving the NP object to the left by itself, as in (31), is ok, indicating the NP is a unit, but moving the particle and the NP together is not ok, as (32) shows, indicating they do not form a phrase:

27. She put down — the customers.
28. *She put — down the customers.
29. She put down the customers and the owner.
30. *She put down the customers and down the owner.
31. It was the customers she put down.
32. *It was down the customers she put.

In (33) and (34), examples are given of phrasal verbs without an NP object:

33. His career is taking off.
34. They finally gave in.

Because the verb and particle have lost their independent meanings, just like the verbs in (15) to (25) above, they are referred to as phrasal verbs. Unlike the phrasal verbs in (15) to (25), they lack objects. Some other examples are *sleep in, turn in*, as in (35):

35. Even though I turned in early last night, I slept in.

4. Phrasal prepositional verbs (Optional)

Constructions with phrasal prepositional verbs combine a verb, a particle, a preposition, and an NP. The object of such a verb is a prepositional object, as indicated with brackets in (36) and (37) for the verbs *put up with* and *come up with*:

36. Orrmm will not put up [with that noise].
37. Benji came up [with a new solution to Fermat's Theorem].

The reason they are phrasal is that the verb and the particle have lost their independent meaning. They are, however, not very prepositional since the preposition and the prepositional object cannot be passivized very well, as the awkwardness of (38) shows. Nevertheless, they are called phrasal prepositional:

38. ?That noise will not be put up with.

Other examples are *cut down on, catch up on, get away with, stand up for, face up to,* and *check up on.*

5.   Objects and adverbials

As a possible help in distinguishing the different functions, Table 5.1 is provided.

Table 5.1. Differences among Objects, Su/Obj Predicates, and Adverbials

	Objects	Su/Obj Predicates	Adverbials
Obligatory	yes	yes	no: optional info on time, place, manner, etc.
Passive	yes	no	no

I have already mentioned that adverbials are optional but that objects and predicates are not. A second criterion for distinguishing the different functions is passivization. As mentioned, direct and indirect objects and the NP in the prepositional object can be passivized, e.g. (39), (40), and (41) respectively:

39. Emma was seen.
40. Walter was given a book.
41. The article was referred to.

Not yet mentioned above is that objects of phrasal verbs can also be passivized, as expected if they are objects. An example is (42):

42. The scandal was covered up immediately.

The NPs in adverbials, subject predicates, and object predicates cannot be passivized, as is shown for adverbials in (43) and object predicates in (44):

43. *The meeting was slept during.
44. *The chair was elected him. (passivized from *We elected him chair*)

As expected, the direct object in (44) can be passivized namely as *He was elected the chair.*

So, in contrast to prepositional objects such as those in (8) and (9) above, in a sentence with an adverbial PP such as (45), the adverbial PP can be left out, as in (46). Sentences with an adverbial cannot be passivized by making the NP *the meeting* into a subject, as shown in (43), unlike the ones with prepositional and phrasal objects, as in (41) and (42) above respectively, where the NP can become subject:

45. He slept [during the meeting].
46. He slept.

In the previous chapter, we discussed intransitive verbs such as *sleep, sneeze, go,* and *swim.* Now that we know there are PP objects as well as PP adverbials, how can we tell which is which using the criteria from Table 5.1, e.g. in sentences such as (47) and (48):

47. I went [to the library].
48. I swam [in the pool].

Some speakers regard the information contained in the PP as essential and others consider it less so. If the goal of the going is seen as obligatory in (47), one might call the PP an object, a prepositional object in this case; if the goal is seen as optional, the PP would be an adverbial. Hence, for sentences such as (47) and (48), there are two different analyses: the verbs can be intransitive ones with the PPs functioning as adverbials or the verbs can be prepositional ones with the PPs functioning as prepositional objects. Notice that these sentences differ as to whether or not they can be passivized, as shown in (49) and (50). Testing if passivization occurs or not makes the adverbial analysis plausible for (47); and the object analysis for (52):

49. *The library was gone to.
50. ?The pool was swum in.

Those of you for whom (49) and/or (50) are ok consider both or one of the adverbials more like objects. Such slight differences between speakers are possible.

It could be that (50) sounds awkward because speakers feel ill at ease with the participle of the verb *swim.* Let's therefore try two other sentences and their passives:

51. He walked on the grass.
52. Washington slept in this bed.
53. The grass was walked on.
54. This bed was slept in.

Sentences (53) and (54) provide evidence that *the grass* and *this bed* are real objects.

Two other frequently asked questions are (a) how the object predicate, as in (55) to (57), repeated from Chapter 4, differs from a modifier to a noun, e.g. *from Mars* in (58), or (b) from an adverbial in (59). I have indicated the most likely analyses by means of brackets:

55. She painted [the house] [purple].
56. Jane considers [Pride and Prejudice] [a classic].
57. She put [the cup] [on the table].
58. I saw [a man from Mars].
59. I saw [a man] [in the garden].

The answer is that, in (58), *from Mars* forms part of the direct object (as indicated by the brackets) which can be replaced by a single element, as in (60). In a sentence such as (57), *on the table* is not part of the direct object since they cannot both be replaced by one element as the ungrammatical (61) shows:

60. I saw him.
61. *She put it.

The same is true for (56), since (62) has quite a different meaning than (56):

62. Jane considers it.

Taking the object predicate away in (55), however, does not result in such a different sentence, but here I would argue *purple* is a real object complement since, unlike in (58), *house purple* is not one unit, and unlike *in the garden* in (59), *purple* says nothing about where, when, or how the painting took place.

6.   Conclusion

As a conclusion, I list instances of the eight types of verbs we have discussed in Chapters 4 and 5.

Table 5.2. Verb types

Name	Example	Complement	Sentence
intransitive	swim, arrive	–	She arrived (early).
(mono)transitive	see, eat, read	Direct Object	She saw me.
ditransitive	give, tell	Direct and Indirect Object	I gave him flowers.
copula	be, become	Subject Predicate	She is nice.
complex transitive	consider, know	Direct Object and Object Predicate	I consider her nice.
prepositional	refer, glance	Prepositional Object	He glanced at the book
phrasal	switch on/give in	Direct Object/–	She turned off the light He gave in.
phrasal prepositional	get down to	Prepositional Object	He got down to business.

Typically, the direct and indirect objects are realized as NPs and the subject and object predicates as AdjPs, but as was indicated above, there are other possibilities. The prepositional object is always a PP.

Adverbials are not relevant for the classification of verbs since they can always be added or deleted. As mentioned above, they are typically realized as PPs and AdvPs even though NPs and clauses are also possible. As an addition to Table 4.2 where the functions of NP, VP, and AdjP are given, Table 5.3 does the same for PP and AdvP. Notice how versatile the PP is.

Table 5.3. The functions of PPs and AdvPs

		> Indirect Object (*give it [to him]*)
Subject Predicate (*is [in the garden]*) <	PP	> Prepositional Object (*insist [on it]*)
Object Predicate (*put it [in the car]*) <		> Adverbial (*swim [during the day]*)
	AdvP >	Adverbial (*swim [carefully]*)

Key terms are **adverbial, prepositional and phrasal verbs,** (don't worry too much about phrasal prepositional verbs), **VP- and S-adverbials.**

Exercises

A. Identify the functions in (63) to (68). Draw trees for (63) and (66):

   63. Fortunately, she found it easily.
   64. I separated it carefully.
   65. She found it easy.
   66. He baked Zoya bread last night (i.e. he baked it for her).
   67. Wisely, the pig from Mars left relatively early.
   68. The hard-working students seemed exhausted after three weeks of classes.

B. Find the adverbials in the text below (adapted from an Amnesty International document). How are they realized, i.e. what kind of phrases are they? Be careful not to list the phrases that modify nouns (*of the failure of justice*) or adjectives.
Are there prepositional objects? Are there phrasal verbs?

> The organization provides a number of instances of the failure of justice in this report. The government authorities have failed to address the problem of 'disappearances' in Punjab. The government has not responded to any of the cases documented since December. The practice of ignoring petitions continues.
>
> The Supreme Court found the police guilty of abducting and killing people but grave concerns remain unaddressed. The report expresses concern about recent allegations in the press that hundreds of people have been killed. Continuing allegations of 'disappearances' are indicative of the absence of a serious commitment by the state authorities.

C. Take a verb and combine it with different prepositions and explain what kind of verb is the result. For instance, take *sleep*, combine it with *in, during, off, around, over, outside*.

D. What do (69) and (70) tell you about *switch on* and *look up* respectively:

   69. It was the light he switched on.
   70. *I looked up the word and up the quote.

E. Make a sentence containing the verb *complain about*. What kind of verb is it? Do the same with *resort to, comment on*, and *catch up with*.

F. Explain the ambiguity in the cartoon below:

Reprinted by permission of Johnny Hart and Creators Syndicate, Inc.

G. How would you describe the difference between 'to visit with somebody' and 'to visit somebody'? Speakers of English use both. What would you say?

H. In the short text below, identify the underlined verbs (e.g. intransitive, complex transitive) and the function of the phrases in brackets:

> I have [a shocking news item]. [This little-known tidbit] will stun some of you and put the rest [in a catatonic haze]. This is why I am warning you to brace yourselves. The Olympics are going on [right now].

> (adapted from a piece by Steve Galindo in the ASU State Press)

I. Do the same in the text below. How would you analyze *deal* in the last sentence?

> Underground nitrogen leak shuts down roads in the city

> A worker from T&T Construction punctured [a high-pressure nitrogen line] at about 7 a.m., shutting down [traffic] on the northeast side of town [all day]. The Police Department blocked off a large area because [it] didn't [initially] know what was leaking. "[It] could have been natural gas, so we had to be [careful]," [Tena Ray, a spokesperson], said. "Fortunately, we don't have to deal with things like this very often".

> (adapted from a piece by Michelle Beaver in the ASU State Press)

J. Construct a sentence with three adverbials.

Class discussion

K. In connection with phrasal verbs, we discussed intransitive phrasal verbs, such as *take off* and *give in*, repeated here as (71) and (72). *Take off* can also be a transitive phrasal verb as in (73):

71. His career took off.
72. They finally gave in.
73. She took off her glasses.

How would you analyze (74)? If you looked up *away* in a dictionary, it would tell you it derives from the PP *on way* and is now an adverb or preposition, just like *off* and *in*:

74. He went away.

One of the ways to solve this is to see if you can question where he went. If you could, that would mean it would be an adverb, and not a particle. It is not a likely preposition since it has no NP as its sister (which we suggested in Chapter 2 was a way to differentiate between prepositions on the one hand and adverbs and particles on the other).

L. A garbage collection company used (75) as one of its slogans. Explain the ambiguity:

75. Our business is picking up

Keys to the Exercises

A. Adv Su Pred DO Adv
    Su Pred DO Adv
    Su Pred DO ObPred
    Su Pred IO DO Adv
    Adv Su Pred Adv
    Su Pred SuPred Adv

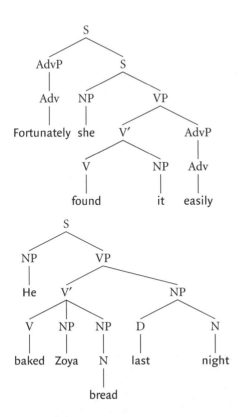

B. Adverbials: *in this report*: PP; *since December*: PP; *in Punjab*: PP. Note that the latter is ambiguous and could also be the modifier of *disappearances*. *Respond* could be argued to be prepositional. There are no phrasal verbs.

C. *Sleep in* would be an intransitive phrasal, with *in* a particle, since *in* does not have it original (locational) meaning. *Sleep around* is similar. *Sleep off* is a transitive phrasal since one can say *sleep off a hangover* and *sleep it off*; *off* is a particle, because you would have to look up the meaning in a dictionary. *Sleep during* consists of an intransitive verb *sleep* and a preposition *during*. *During* is not a particle since *sleep it during* is ungrammatical, and it is not an adverb since it cannot occur independently of an NP, as in *I slept during*. *Sleep outside* contains an intransitive verb *sleep* and an adverb *outside*.

D. – Because *the light* is preposed in (69) without taking *on* along, *on the light* is not a unit that functions as an adverbial. In addition, since one can say *switch it on* the verb is phrasal and not prepositional.
    – *Up the word* is not a unit in (70) since it cannot be coordinated with a

similar unit. Also, one can say *look it up*, indicating *look up* is phrasal.

E. She complained about the government; He resorted to violence; They commented on the book. They are all prepositional object verbs.
    A sentence with the phrasal prepositional verb 'catch up with' is: They caught up with him.

F. The ambiguity is due to 'forever' being either an adverb, or a preposition and a noun 'ever'.

G. 'To visit with somebody' is said to be American English, whereas 'to visit somebody' is said to be British English. The difference is that in the former case, *visit with* is a prepositional verb, whereas in the latter case, *visit* is a (mono)transitive verb.

H. I have: transitive [a shocking news item: DO]. [This little-known tidbit: Su] will stun: transitive some of you and put: complex transitive the rest [in a catatonic haze: ObjPred]. This is: copula why I am warning: transitive you to brace: transitive yourselves. The Olympics are going on: intransitive phrasal [right now: adverbial].

I. A worker from T&T Construction punctured: transitive [a high-pressure nitrogen line: DO] at about 7 a.m., shutting down: (transitive) phrasal [traffic: DO] on the northeast side of town [all day: adverbial]. The Police Department blocked off: (transitive) phrasal a large area because [it: Su] didn't [initially: adverbial] know: transitive what was leaking: intransitive. "[It: Su] could have been: copula natural gas, so we had to be [careful: Su Predicate]," [Tena Ray, a spokesperson: Su (appositive)], said. "Fortunately, we don't have to deal with things like this very often".
    Deal is a verb taking a prepositional object.

J. [This morning], I left [early] [because otherwise the traffic is hopeless].

Special topic: The split infinitive

Infinitives are non-finite verbs. The infinitival marker *to* is not a preposition but an infinitive marker and is therefore seen as belonging to the Verb Group (see next chapter).

The Rule: "Do not separate an infinitival verb from its accompanying *to*, as in *to boldly go where* …".

Swan (1980:327) writes: "[s]plit infinitive structures are quite common in English, especially in an informal style. A lot of people consider them 'bad style', and avoid them if possible, placing the adverb before the *to*, or in end-position in the sentence". Fowler (1926 [1950]:558) writes:

> [t]he English-speaking world may be divided into (1) those who neither know nor care what a split infinitive is; (2) those who do not know but care very much; (3) those who know & condemn; (4) those who know & approve; & (5) those who know & distinguish.

Fowler himself disapproves of the use of the split infinitive. Quirk & Greenbaum (1973:312) remark:

> [t]he inseparability of *to* from the infinitive is ... asserted in the widely held opinion that it is bad style to 'split the infinitive'. Thus rather than: '?He was wrong to *suddenly* leave the country' many people (especially in BrE) prefer: 'He was wrong to leave the country suddenly'. It must be acknowledged, however, that in some cases the 'split infinitive' is the only tolerable ordering, since avoiding the 'split infinitive' results in clumsiness or ambiguity.

Some examples of the split infinitive, from 1200 on, are (76) to (83). Would you change these? If so, how?

76. I want somebody who will be on there not to legislate from the bench but **to** faithfully **interpret** the constitution. (George Bush, quoted in *The Economist*, 6 July 1991)
77. Remember **to** always **footnote** the source. (from a computer magazine)
78. [This] will make it possible for everyone **to** gently **push up** the fees. (NYT, 21 July 1991)
79. ...to get the Iraqis **to** peacefully **surrender**... (NYT, 7 July 1991)
80. Layamon *Brut* Otho, 6915 (early 13th century)
    fo[r] to londes **seche**, 'for to countries seek'.
81. *Cursor Mundi* (Ld MS) 18443, (early 14th century)
    Blessid be þou lord off hevyn ... Synfull men **for to** þus **lede** in paradice, 'sinful men for to thus lead in paradise'.
82. Wyclif, *Matthew* 5, 34 (late 14th century)
    Y say to ȝou, **to** nat **swere** on al manere,
    'I say to you to not curse in all ways'.

83.   *Apology for the Lollards* 57 (late 14th century)
       Poul seiþ, þu þat prechist **to** not **steyl**, stelist,
       'Paul says, you who preach to not steal steal'.

In the discussion on the Verb Group that follows in the next chapter I am not including the split infinitive. As mentioned in the preface, I am not completely happy with the analysis in Chapter 6, but giving an alternative structure would lead too far away from the central parts.

6 The structure of the Verb Group in the VP

In this chapter, the structure of the verb in the VP is discussed in more detail. Most of the sentences we have talked about so far have contained one (finite lexical) verb. In English, a sentence can (in principle) have four auxiliaries and a lexical verb. English is quite unusual in this respect, compared to other languages that typically do not have this many auxiliaries. This complex of auxiliaries and the lexical verb will be called the Verb Group, abbreviated in the tree as VGP (and used when auxiliaries are present). English is also unusual in that if an auxiliary is not present and the sentence is negative or a question, a 'dummy' auxiliary *do* is needed.

In this chapter, the auxiliaries are defined and characterized (see Table 6.1). A label is given to each of the auxiliaries, but in the tree structure I represent auxiliaries as part of the Verb Group. Thus, the Verb Group will be flat, i.e. non-hierarchical (for alternatives, see further reading). Auxiliaries are associated with a particular ending, i.e. affix, that appears on the verb immediately to their right (see Table 6.3). This process is called affix-hop. This chapter will also provide rules for identifying finite verbs and for distinguishing them from non-finite verbs.

1. Auxiliary verbs

Verbs can be divided into **lexical** and **auxiliary verbs**. A VP contains one lexical verb and (optionally) up to four auxiliaries. In Chapter 2, we talked about the distinction between verbs and auxiliaries in terms of lexical as opposed to grammatical. Most of the VPs dealt with in the previous chapters consisted of a single verb, and then they automatically are lexical verbs. Examples of lexical verbs are *arrive, see, walk,* copula *be,* transitive *do,* etc. They carry a real meaning and are not dependent on another verb. In addition to a lexical verb, the VP may contain auxiliaries. Auxiliaries depend on another verb, add grammatical information, and are grouped together with the lexical verb in a Verb Group.

Auxiliaries are also sometimes called helping verbs since they help out other verbs. For instance, in (1), *have* does not mean *possess*; it merely indicates that the action of the lexical verb *see* was in the past. In (2), on the other hand, *have* has a lexical meaning ('to possess') and there is no other verb present:

1. The Malacandran has seen the hross.
2. I have a book on sentences.

Unlike lexical verbs, auxiliaries invert in questions, as in (3), can precede the negative *n't* (i.e. the common form of *not*), as in (4), and can be used in tag questions, as in (5):

3. Has she gone yet?
4. She hasn't done that yet.
5. She hasn't done that yet, has she?

The Verb Group will be represented as a flat tree structure, as in (6). As mentioned in Chapter 3, grammatical categories such as the auxiliary do not have their own phrase (in this book) and hence do not function at sentence level. Grammatical categories function inside a phrase or, in this case, inside the Verb Group (if auxiliaries are present, VGP will be used; otherwise, V will suffice):

6.

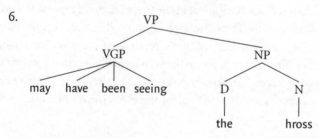

If *n't/not* appears, as in (4) and (5), this will be included in the Verb Group as well. Table 6.1 provides some ways to recognize auxiliaries:

Table 6.1. Characteristics of auxiliary verbs

a.	They must be used with a lexical verb (unless ellipsis occurs)
b.	They have little meaning; rather, they express tense and aspect
c.	They invert in questions, as in (3)
d.	They occur before *n't*, as in (4)
e.	They are used as tags, as in (5)

1.1 Modals

English is exceptional in the numbers of auxiliaries it has and the combinations it allows. Each auxiliary has its own name and position in regard to the others. Modals do not have agreement or tense endings (hence *he cans; *I am canning to go); they are the first to occur in a sequence of auxiliaries; and do not require an ending, i.e. affix, on the verb following them (He can walk, but not: *He can walked). Thus, (7) is a typical instance: the modal could is first and the next verb be does not have an affix:

7.   Rigobertha could be going tomorrow.

There are nine modals in English: can, could, may, might, shall, should, will, would, and must. Modal auxiliaries express uncertainty, as in (7) and (8), necessity (must, should), ability, as in (9), permission, as in (10):

8.   It might snow.
9.   I can swim.
10.   You may go now.

They are also used where some languages would use the subjunctive mood. The Modern English subjunctive is very restricted. Examples are given in (11) and (12), but since they are not common, I will not go into this more deeply:

11.   I wish it were Friday.
12.   They insisted that he go.

Modals are often used when we ask a favor of someone, as in (13), or when we want to be polite. The 'past' form (could) in (13) is seen as more polite than the 'present' form (can) in (14). Modals have lost the ability to express present and past tense, but they are finite. Thus, the difference between (13) and (14) is not related to when the action happened, but to how likely the event is to happen. Could is more polite since it expresses a more remote possibility; can is more direct and hence seen as less polite:

13.   Could I borrow some money?
14.   Can I borrow some money?

In English, the modal will (and shall in some varieties of English) is used to express future, as in (15) and (16), the latter of which is the contracted form:

15.   He will go to Mars next year.
16.   She'll walk on Jupiter next year.

There are special modals, called semi-modals: *dare (to), need (to), have to, ought to*. They are seen as modals since they express obligation, ability, and necessity. *Used to* is sometimes added to this group, but it is much more a regular auxiliary expressing habituality. Semi-modals are in flux between auxiliary and lexical verb status. Thus, in (17), T.S. Eliot uses *dare* as a lexical verb, but in (18), acceptable for some speakers, *dare* is not a lexical verb but an auxiliary:

17. Shall I part my hair behind? Do I dare to eat a peach?
     (The Love Song of J. Alfred Prufock, I 122)
18. Dare I eat a peach?

Dare in (18) is an auxiliary because it moves to the front of the sentence to form a question (see Chapter 4 where we used this rule to find the subject; see Chapter 11 for a structure). In English, only auxiliaries move, and if the sentence contains just a lexical verb, a dummy *do* will be used (see Section 1.5). Since *do* is used in (17), it is usually thought that *dare* in (17) is a lexical verb. Some people use (18) in very formal situations. The other semi-modals allow a variety of constructions as well. For instance, *ought* in (19) is very much an auxiliary since it moves, but in (20), it is not. Both occur in 19th century texts (see the Oxford English Dictionary):

19. Robert Browning, Agamemnon 796
     How ought I address thee, how ought I revere thee?
20. He didn't ought to go.

In class, we will go through several options for these auxiliaries.

1.2 Perfect *have*

Have is the perfect auxiliary. It does not make the meaning perfective or finished though. It is used to indicate that a past action still has relevance. For instance, in (21), the speaker still lives here:

21. I have lived here for ages.

When *have* is used, the next verb (if it is regular) is marked with an -*ed* ending, e.g. *lived* in (21), through 'affix-hop'. The form of the verb that is the result of affix-hop is called the past participle, or *ed*-participle. The term past participle is perhaps somewhat confusing since, e.g. in (21), the presence of the past participle does not make the entire sentence past tense. In (22), the ending related to *have* appears on *be*, which is an irregular verb (like *see, go, do,* etc.):

22. Zoltan may have been playing a terrible game.

1.3 Progressive *be*

The progressive indicates that the action is or was in progress, as in (23) and (24). This is called the aspect of a verb, as opposed to the tense of a verb which tells you whether the action took place in the present, past, or future. In (23) to (25), the aspect is progressive, but the tense is present in (23), past in (24), and future in (25). Since the progressive indicates that an action is or was in progress, it is incompatible with verbs that express a state, as shown in (26) and (27):

23. Zoya is walking.
24. Zoltan was playing the piano, when a noise disturbed him.
25. He will be walking the dog.
26. *He is knowing the answer.
27. *The book is being blue.

To form the progressive, a form of *to be* is used, as in (23). The verb that follows has an *-ing* ending through affix-hop, and is called a present participle, or *ing*-participle. Again, as in the case of past participles, the term is confusing since the presence of the present participle need not make the sentence into the present tense, as (24) shows. The verb *to be* is the most irregular in 'standard' English, and for ease of reference, I provide the forms in Table 6.2.

Table 6.2. Forms of *to be*

	Present	Past
I	am	was
s/he, it	is	was
we, you, they	are	were

Some people argue that sometimes the forms of *be* are not auxiliary verbs but lexical ones, and that the *-ing* forms are adjectives. I mention it here as a possible analysis in some cases. For instance in (23) above, one could argue *walking* is like *nice*, since like *nice*, it can be used to modify a noun in (28):

28. My nice walking shoes are very light.

My own feeling is that *walking* in (23), where it refers to an action, is very different from *walking* in (28), where it describes the qualities of a noun. If we considered the distinctions made in Chapter 2, *walking* would be a verb in (23), but an adjective in (28). The same ambiguity occurs with passives, as will be shown in 1.4.

1.4 Passive *be*

As seen in Chapter 4, passive constructions, as in (29b), are made from active ones, as in (29a), by switching the subject and the object around and by adding a form of *to be*. The verb immediately following this *be* has a past participle ending, in this case *-n*, because of the affix hopping from the auxiliary to the next verb:

29.　a.　I see him.
　　　b.　He is seen by me.

The stylistic effects of passives will be discussed in Chapter 11. For now, some comments on the form suffice. In (30a), the Verb Group consists of a modal, a perfect, and a lexical verb. Because of the perfect *have*, the form of the verb *see* is a past participle. In (30b), the passive *be* is added and now its form is that of past participle (namely *been*) because it follows *have*. *Seen* appears as past participle as well because it follows the passive *be*. If this sounds too complex, just look at the ending of the verb on the immediate right of the auxiliary and Table 6.3 below:

30.　a.　Zoya may have seen Zoltan.
　　　b.　Zoltan may have been seen by Zoya.

Passive participles can often be analyzed as adjectives (*known, mixed, written*) and are then not part of the Verb Group. Then, the form of *be* is not an auxiliary either, but a copula. It is up to the reader to decide whether *delighted* in (31) is a passive participle or an adjective. Most linguists would argue that (31) is not a passive construction since (a) adding a *by*-phrase, as in (32), is awkward, and (b) *delighted* appears after copula verbs such as *seem*, as in (33), which is typical of adjectives (see Chapter 3):

31.　She was delighted to get chocolate.
32.　*She was delighted by Edward to get chocolate.
33.　She seemed delighted to get chocolate.

As we'll see in section 2, if there are two *be* auxiliaries in a row, the second one is the passive auxiliary. Note that the latter auxiliary gets the affix of the preceding one through affix-hop, in this case that of the progressive. *Seen* is a past participle because of the preceding passive *be*:

34. He may be being seen.

1.5 The dummy *do*

Lexical verbs, such as *know* cannot be used in questions and negative sentences, as (35) and (36) show:

35. *Knows he not the answer?
36. *He knows not the answer

To form a question or a negative, dummy *do* is needed. *Do* does not appear together with the other auxiliaries but is typically only inserted in questions, as in (37), or negative sentences with *n't/not*, as in (38), or for emphasis, as in (39). This *do* only occurs if the sentence does not contain a regular auxiliary, hence the name 'dummy':

37. Does he know the answer?
38. He does not know the answer.
39. Oh, but I DID know the answer.

In earlier English, dummy *do* does not appear in this way. In Shakespeare's time, for instance, (40) to (42) were quite common as well:

40. 2 Henry IV, IV, 1, 98
    Or if it were, it not belongs to you
41. Hamlet, I, i, 55
    What think you on't?
42. Hamlet, III, i, 106
    What meanes your Lordship?

2. The order of auxiliaries and affix hop

The auxiliaries dealt with in Sections 1.1 to 1.4 occur in a particular order: modal, perfect, progressive, and passive. Since dummy *do* only occurs if no other auxiliary is present, I will ignore it here. As mentioned, the verb that immediately follows a particular auxiliary bears the ending, also called affix, of that auxiliary. Since the affix associated with a particular auxiliary does not appear on the auxiliary but on the next verb, this process is called affix-hop. The auxiliaries and affixes are listed in the table below (please note that irregular past participles are not listed, e.g. the intransitives *swum, lain*):

Table 6.3. Auxiliaries and their affixes

Name	Auxiliary	Affix that appears on the next verb
Modal:	modal	–
perfect:	have	ed/en
progressive:	be	ing
passive:	be	ed/en

A sentence that includes all four types of auxiliaries sounds a little contrived:

43. That thief may have been being observed.

In (43), there is a modal *may*, a perfect *have*, a progressive *be* marked with *-en* because of *have*, a passive *be* marked with *-ing* because of the progressive immediately to its left, and a lexical verb *observe* that bears the affix of the passive auxiliary immediately to its left.

As shown in (6) above, the structure of a sentence with a number of auxiliaries is not very insightful, i.e. it is very flat, since all the auxiliaries are part of the Verb Group. The negative adverb *not* in English must be included in the Verb Group as well since it is an affix on the finite auxiliary. A structure for (44) is (45):

44. He hasn't been doing his homework.

45.

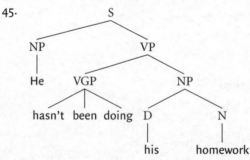

Other structures have been suggested with a less flat structure (see further reading) but they are still controversial and would lead us into a new set of arguments.

3. Finiteness

The sentences we have discussed so far have been complete sentences, not sentence fragments. A complete sentence consists of a subject and a finite verb. A finite verb agrees with the subject (in the present tense) and indicates present or past. Its subject is nominative, which can only be seen in the case of pronouns in Modern English, i.e. the subject pronoun of finite verbs must be nominative *I, you, he, she, it, we* and *they*, not accusative *me, him, her, us* or *them* (*you* and *it* are both nominative and accusative).

Finite sentences such as (45) have a Verb Group with a finite verb as its first (or only) member. In (46), *have* is the finite verb that makes the entire Verb Group finite and as a result the sentence is finite:

46. I [have been going] there frequently.

Have is finite because it shows subject agreement (*have* rather than *has*, as in (47)), indicates present tense (*have* rather than *had*, as in (48)), and has a nominative subject (*I* rather than *me*, as in the ungrammatical (49)):

47. He has been going there frequently.
48. He had been going there frequently.
49. *Me have been going there frequently.

Note that in some varieties of English (49) is grammatical.

Modals, as in (50), are finite even though (for historical reasons) they never display subject-verb agreement:

50. I might have done that.

Only finite sentences are complete sentences. Sentence (52) below is not a complete sentence but is a sentence fragment. Most of us, however, use fragments in informal speech, in poetry, e.g. John Keats in (51), or even in writing:

51. Ode on a Grecian Urn
Thou still unravish'd bride of quietness!
Thou foster-child of silence and slow time,

...

What mad pursuit? What struggle to escape?
What pipes and timbrels? What wild ecstacy?

...

Nevertheless, they are generally frowned upon in formal writing. How can (52) be fixed?

52.   Mentioning that point about finite sentences yesterday.

Sentence (52) can become a full sentence by adding a subject and a finite verb as in (53):

53.   I was mentioning that point about finite sentences yesterday.

As will be shown in a later chapter, non-finite sentences can only be part of other sentences. How many lexical verbs are there in (54)? Which are the finite Verb Groups?

54.   I have heard her sing too often.

In (54), there are two lexical verbs, *heard* and *sing*, but only the first Verb Group is finite since *have* is finite (e.g. the subject of *have* is nominative *I* whereas the subject of the non-finite *sing* is accusative *her*). Other sentences that include a non-finite Verb Group are (55) and (56), with the non-finite Verb Groups in bold. Note that the infinitive marker *to* is part of the Verb Group:

55.   **Seeing** the beautiful sunset in her rearview mirror, she missed her exit.
56.   She forgot completely **to go** to the store.

In (55), *seeing* and *missed* are lexical verbs, but only *missed* is finite. In (56), *forgot* and *go* are the lexical verbs, but only *forgot* is finite.

A sentence can contain many Verb Groups, a (potentially) limitless number if, as mentioned in Chapter 1, the speaker had enough energy and could continue (57). Sentences such as (57), containing more than one Verb Group, are discussed in Chapters 7 and 10:

57.   I noticed that she mentioned that he was saying that she should tell him ...

Imperatives are used to order someone to do something. They often lack a subject, as in (58), but this need not be the case, as (59) shows:

58.   Draw the trees for these sentences.
59.   You, draw trees for this.

Imperatives are complete sentences and not sentence fragments.

4. Conclusion

In summary, this chapter has classified the different kinds of auxiliary verbs: the modal, perfect, progressive, and passive which occur in this order; *do* is added in questions and negative sentences when an auxiliary is not available. Finiteness is discussed: a verb is finite if it agrees with the subject and if this subject bears nominative case. Since finite verbs and their relationship to lexical and auxiliary verbs are often challenging, I end with a list of examples in Table 6.4. The clauses are indicated by brackets but their use will not be explained till the next chapter. For now, remember that if you have a lexical verb, there is a clause:

Table 6.4. The relationship between finite (in **bold**) and lexical/AUXiliary verb (underlined).

60. [Those people   **could**   have   been underline{sightseeing}].
                AUX   AUX   AUX lexical
                modal   perfect progressive

61. He **has**   been   wanting [to go there for ages]].
      AUX   AUX   lexical   lexical
      perfect progressive

62. [I **mentioned** [that it   **had** been said [that she   wanted [to leave]]]].
   lexical   AUX AUX lexical   lexical   lexical
                      perfect passive

63. [I **saw** [him   leaving]].
   lexical   lexical

64. [[Feeling fine], he **left** early].
   lexical   lexical

In table 6.4, I have not underlined *to*, but it can be seen as an auxiliary.

Key terms are **auxiliary and lexical verb; affix; participle; modal, perfect, progressive, and passive; finite and non-finite; nominative case and tense.**

Exercises

A. Identify the auxiliary/ies in (65) to (68), e.g. are they passive, or modal?:

65. Rigobertha has been meeting Carlos.
66. Belo and Horta were awarded the Nobel Peace Prize.
67. Indonesia was not too happy with the decision.
68. They may be bringing about a peaceful solution in Nepal.

B. Identify the auxiliaries (e.g. modal, passive) in the passage from Chapter 4, repeated here:

> Granny was waiting at the door of the apartment. She looked small, lonely, and patient, and at the sight of her the children and their mother felt instantly guilty. Instead of driving straight home from the airport, they had stopped outside Nice for ice cream. They might have known how much those extra twenty minutes would mean to Granny.

C. Think up a sentence with a perfect and a passive auxiliary.
Add a progressive auxiliary to: *He might go.* Now add a perfect as well.

D. Take out the perfect in (69):

69. He could have been going.

E. Identify the auxiliaries and verbs that are **finite** in A and B above.

F. Read the two poems below. Then, compare the use of the verbs: lexical as opposed to auxiliary, and finite as opposed to non-finite. What is the effect of this different verb use?

As the cat	Fire and Ice
climbed over	
the top of	Some say the world will end in fire,
	Some say in ice.
the jamcloset	From what I've tasted of desire
first the right	I hold with those who favor fire.
forefoot	
	But if it had to perish twice,
carefully	I think I know enough of hate
then the hind	To say that for destruction ice
stepped down	Is also great
	And would suffice.
into the pit of	
the empty	Robert Frost (1874–1963)
flowerpot	
william carlos williams	
(1883–1963)	

Keys to the Exercises

A. *has* (perfect) and *been* (progressive) in (65); *were* (passive) in (66); none in (67); *may* (modal) and *be* (progressive) in (68).

B. Granny was (progressive) waiting at the door of the apartment. She looked small, lonely, and patient, and at the sight of her the children and their mother felt instantly guilty. Instead of driving straight home from the airport, they had (perfect) stopped outside Nice for ice cream. They might (modal) have (perfect) known how much those extra twenty minutes would (modal) mean to Granny.

C. He has been seen.
    He might be going.
    He might have been going.

D. He could be going.

E. In (65), *has*; in (66), *were*; in (67), *was*; in (68), *may*. In the text, *was, looked, felt, had, might, would*.

F. In the first poem, there are 2 finite lexical verbs; in the second, there are 12 lexical and 4 auxiliary verbs, and only 1 Verb Group is non-finite. Note also that in the second poem, a number of nouns are somewhat verbal, e.g. *hate, destruction, fire, desire*. They are either based on a verb or can be used as a verb. Discuss the effects of the verb use on the tone of the poems.

Special topic: Reduction of *have* and the shape of participles

The prescriptive rule can be formulated as follows: "In formal writing, do not contract auxiliaries".

Most people do not fully spell out the auxiliaries in speech or informal writing. Thus, *have* in (70) becomes *'ve* or *a*, as in (71), or even *of*, as in (72):

70. I should have done that sooner.
71. I shoulda done that sooner.
72. I should of done that sooner.

Reduction of *have* is typically done by speakers when *have* is in fact an auxiliary as in (71) and (72), not when it is a main verb, as in (73), formed from (74):

73. *He shoulda books in his office.
74. He should have books in his office.

Reduction of auxiliaries has occurred since medieval times. Sentences (75) to (79) are from the 15th and 16th centuries, and the reduced forms of *have* are in bold:

75. *Paston Letters,* #131 (1449)
    it xuld **a** be seyd
    'It should have been said'.
76. Idem, #176 (1464)
    ʒe wold **a** be plesyd
    'You would have been pleased'.
77. Idem, #205 (1469)
    there xuld not **a** be do so mykele
    'There should not have been done so much'.
78. Shakespeare, *Hamlet,* IV, 5, 65 (First Folio Edition 1623)
    So would I **ha** done by yonder Sunne.
79. Shakespeare, 2 Henry 4, II, 1, 126
    I know you **ha'** practised vpon the easie-yeelding spirit of this woman.

Hence, even though the reduction of *have* to *of* and *-a* is common in speech nowadays (and was common in writing in earlier times), it is now not done in formal writing.

As mentioned, the perfect auxiliary *have* and the passive auxiliary *be* are followed by a past participle. This rule is often violated. Remember the discussion of *lie* and *lay* (with participles as *lain* and *laid* respectively) in Chapter 4? Other instances are the past participles *bitten* and *gone.* They are often replaced by the past tense, as in (80) and (81), but this use is not prescriptively correct in Modern English even though it occurs in writers such as Milton, as in (82), Dryden, Pope, Addison, and Swift (see Finegan 1980: 25–6):

80. Some mosquito has bit me.
81. I should have went to Medical School at the U of A [University of Arizona]. (overheard on ASU campus)
82. *Paradise Lost,* X, 517–8
    According to his doom: he would have spoke,
    But hiss for hiss return'd with forked tongue.

In earlier stages of English, the affix was often not present, as in (83) and (84):

83. Chaucer, *Miller's Tale*, 3739
     What have I do?
84. Idem, *Wife of Bath's Prol.* 7
     If I so ofte myghte have ywedded be.

Review Chapters 4–6

I'll start with Chapter 6. In this chapter, the Verb Group is examined more carefully: a Verb Group contains at least a lexical verb but can also contain one or more auxiliaries. Verbs (and Verb Groups) are either finite or non-finite. If verbs express tense and have a nominative subject, they are finite; if not, they are non-finite.

In Chapters 4 and 5, functions at sentence level are discussed: subject, direct object, indirect object, phrasal object, prepositional object, subject predicate, and object predicate. These are obligatory parts of the sentence. Verbs are classified in terms of whether or not they have obligatory complements (see Table 5.1 above). In contrast, adverbials function to add background and can be added to a sentence optionally and without limitation (except for the speaker's and hearer's level of patience and memory). The difference between direct object, indirect object, phrasal object, and prepositional object on the one hand and subject predicate, object predicate, and adverbial on the other is that the former can be passivized. As a reminder, I'll provide a list of the major verb types with a simple tree for each (see also Table 5.2 above):

1. **Intransitive: no objects**

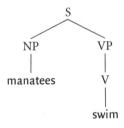

2. **(Mono)transitive: one direct object**

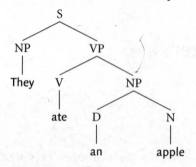

3. **Ditransitive: one direct and one indirect object**

   a.

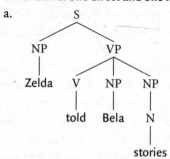

   b.

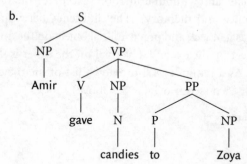

4. **Copula: one subject predicate**

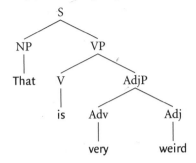

5. **Complex Predicate: one direct object and an object predicate** =

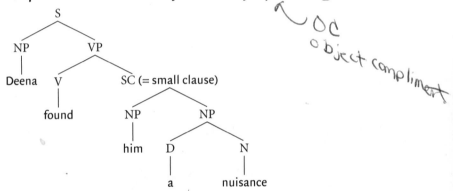

OC
object compliment

6. **Prepositional object verb: one PP object**

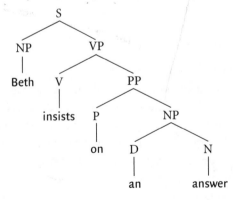

7. **Phrasal: no object if intransitive, as in a; one direct object if transitive, as in b**

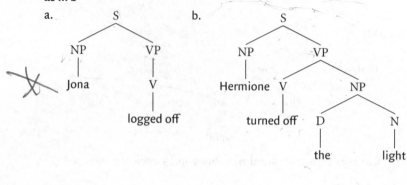

Examples of mid-terms covering Chapter 4–6

Answers are not provided.

In Text A:

A.   Please list the lexical verbs (label them as e.g. transitive, complex transitive, phrasal).

B.   List the adverbials, subjects, and direct objects.

C.   List the auxiliary verbs. Are they modal, perfect, progressive, or passive?

D.   List the finite verbs in the text.

E.   Draw a tree for: Spain was the target at the end of the century

> **Text A** (adapted from: *The Good Neighbor*, by G. Black).
> Ever since the US Civil War, the countries of Central America and the Caribbean have occupied a special place in the American psyche. Cuba, Nicaragua, Panama and their neighbors have been a magnet for adventurers and pioneers, a proving ground for grand abstractions of democracy and freedom, and frequently they have given scoundrels a refuge. For most of the twentieth century people knew them as "banana republics"; by the 1980s, a chain of clothing stores serving affluent customers in today's travel-mad world had adopted that name.
>   This was frontier territory, a land where the whim of the adventurer was often the only law, where Americans had limitless prerogatives, and where people considered outside intruders malicious. Senator Hannegan of Indiana

saw something else. He saw Britain hastening 'with race-horse speed' to seize all of Central America. Spain was the target of similar suspicion at the end of the century, but was succeeded in turn by Germany, Mexico and the Soviet Union. Each of these foreign powers was charged with importing ideologies alien to the natural order of the region.

In Text B

A. Find all the lexical verbs and classify them (monotransitive, phrasal, etc.).

B. Find all the complements and classify them (direct object, indirect object, subject predicate, etc.). How are they realized (NP, PP, AdvP, etc.)?

C. Point out the auxiliary verbs and classify them. Also circle or list the finite verbs.

D. Draw a tree for:
Continued hostilities have resulted in terrible abuses inside Afghanistan.

Text B
Continued hostilities have resulted in catastrophic human rights abuses inside   Z. All warring factions have carried out attacks against residential areas. The factions have targetted civilians and they have killed tens of thousands of people in various parts of the country. The vast majority of the victims have been civilians. Now, the threatened bombardment will leave many people dead and many more wounded.

In Text C

A. Please list and identify the lexical verbs (transitive, intransitive, etc.) and the auxiliary verbs (passive, perfect, etc.) in the first paragraph.

B. Draw a tree for *They met in Paris at the beginning of the 20th century.* Indicate the functions and names/labels.

C. List the finite verbs in the last paragraph.

D. What is the function and name/label (i.e. realization) of the following phrases in the sentences in which they occur:

    a. Picasso's arrival (second paragraph).
    b. a brilliant success (first paragraph).

Text C

New play by Steve Martin hits the mark

Imagine if Steve Martin wrote a comedic concept play with the entirely possible idea that Pablo Picasso and Albert Einstein could have met in Paris at the beginning of the twentieth century in a small bistro. He has succeeded, and the Arizona Theatre Company's production of *Picasso at the Lapin Agile* is a brilliant success. Martin has created a hilarious and thought provoking look at two geniuses.

The play begins with Einstein and several other patrons discussing the probability that Picasso would venture into the bistro. Einstein is anticipating Picasso's arrival. The players discuss everything from physics to the letter 'E'. The play abounds with Steve Martin's bizarre philosophies and even stranger sense of humor.

(adapted from an article in Arizona State University's *State Press*)

E.   Explain (using terminology used in class and in Chapter 5) why the following sentence is ungrammatical:

*Down the president she ran.

F.   Add passive auxiliaries to the following sentences (and make the appropriate changes):

Picasso may have played a part.
Einstein is looking at Picasso.

7 Finite clauses
Embedded and coordinated

So far, the sentences we have focussed on have included one lexical verb and one or more auxiliaries. These are simple sentences. This chapter gives examples of sentences that include more than one lexical verb, which means that they are composed of more than one clause. Sentences that are part of another sentence, i.e. that have a function in that sentence, are often referred to as embedded clauses, and one clause is seen as subordinate to the other. Coordinated sentences are sentences where both clauses are of equal importance. This chapter provides the structure for both types of clauses, making use of the grammatical categories complementizer and coordinator. Both types of constructions enable us to make very long sentences (infinite if we had the energy) and ones we had never heard before. A special kind of sentence, the extraposed one, will also be discussed.

1. Sentences and clauses

A clause contains one lexical verb. Hence, if there are two lexical verbs, there are two clauses. For instance, in (1), the lexical verbs are *noticed* and *like* and hence, there are two clauses: the main clause (*I should have noticed that Zelda does not like Zoltan*) and the embedded one (*Zelda does not like Zoltan*). This can be indicated by means of brackets:

1. [I should have noticed [that Zelda does not like Zoltan]].

Auxiliaries, such as *should, have* and *does,* are not relevant for determining clauses or sentences, only lexical verbs are.

Some linguists call the larger sentence in (1) the sentence or main clause and the smaller sentence the embedded sentence, dependent or subordinate clause. In Section 5, I list some of these terms. I will use both clause and sentence interchangeably to indicate a unit that contains a lexical verb.

The complementizer *that* in (1) functions to link the embedded sentence to the main clause, but can often be left out in English. Other examples of complementizers are *if, whether, because, unless,* and *since.* More on the structure of the embedded clause is given in Section 3.

In (1), both clauses have a VP containing a finite verb, i.e. *should* and *does* (remember auxiliaries can be finite), but embedded sentences can be non-finite as well. In this chapter, I discuss the clauses with finite VPs and in the next those with non-finite VPs. Be careful not to confuse finite verbs, such as *should* or *does,* with lexical verbs, such as *noticed* and *like:* each clause must have a lexical verb, but an (embedded) clause need not have a finite verb.

2.   The functions of clauses

At sentence level, clauses function as subject, direct object, subject predicate, or adverbial. For instance, in (1) above, the clause functions as direct object; in (2), it is a subject; in (3), a subject predicate; and in (4), an adverbial. The clauses are indicated by means of brackets:

2.   [That she left] was nice.
3.   The problem is [that she reads junk].
4.   He read books [because it was required].

Clauses can only function as direct objects, not as indirect objects, objects of phrasal verbs, or prepositional objects (see Chapter 10). They do not function as object predicates either.

Inside an NP or AdjP, clauses function as modifiers (e.g. relative clauses) or complements (e.g. noun complements). Examples of relative clauses will be given in Chapters 9 and 10, and of noun complements in Chapter 10, Section 2.

3.   The structure: S′ (pronounced: S-bar)

As mentioned, embedded sentences have complementizers that connect the embedded clause to another clause. These complementizers are sisters to S, and a sentence with a complementizer is an S′. Using C, S, and S′, a sentence such as (1), slightly simplified by taking the auxiliaries out, has a structure as in (5):

5.

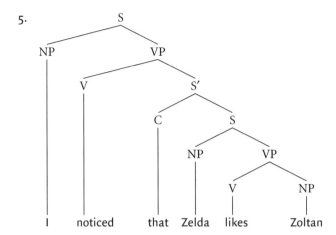

Using an S′ makes it possible to include the complementizer in the sentence and link the embedded S to the main S. In (5), the embedded S′ is the sister to *noticed*, which means that it functions as the direct object to *noticed*.

There are also embedded clauses that express questions. In these, the C position can be occupied by *if*, or by *whether*, as in (6), for which a structure is given in (7). The S′ here, as in (5), functions as a direct object:

6. I asked whether he had seen her.

7.

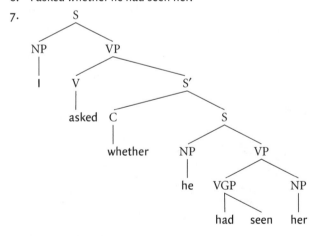

Trees for a subject clause, a subject predicate clause, and an adverbial are given in (8) to (10):

8.

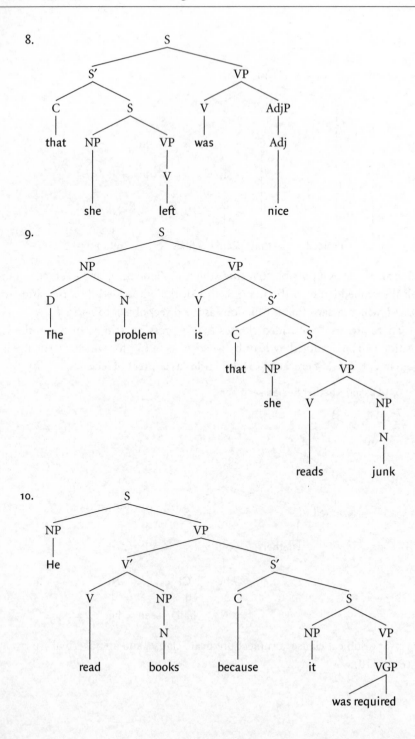

9.

10.

The position of clauses functioning as adverbials, like other kinds of adverbials, is very free. For instance, in a sentence such as (4) above, the *because*-clause can also precede *he read books*, as in (11):

11.   Because it was required, he read books.

We will assume that the tree structure for this is as in a sentence with an S-adverbial as discussed in Chapter 5, namely, as in (12). However, other trees are possible:

12.

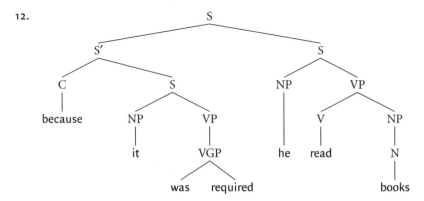

Adverbial clauses may have a preposition as complementizer, as in (13):

13.   She came to the party after he left.

It is not unusual for languages, English included, to have prepositions become complementizers (see the special topic at the end of this chapter).

Sentences such as (2) above are often changed into (14). This is called extraposition. The reason for extraposition is that speakers do not like to have embedded sentences in the beginning or middle of the main clause. The dummy subject *it* takes the place of the extraposed clause:

14.   It was nice that she left.

I'll refrain from drawing a tree here, but if you want to draw one, attach the extraposed S′ as if it were a VP-adverbial.

4. Coordinate sentences

As in the case of coordinate phrases (discussed in Chapter 3), there is a debate over how best to represent sentences such as (15) and (16):

15. She arrived and he left.
16. Phoenix is a city and the moon is made of cheese.

Some people argue that the coordinator *and* really means 'and then' or 'while' and that the second clause is subordinate to the first. If that is the case, the structure of (15) would be similar to the embedded clauses in (10) above, represented as (17), and *and he left* would function as an adverbial to the main clause. Other people argue that the structure is as in (18), where neither clause is subordinate to the other. It really depends on the sentence, e.g. (16) is better represented by (18), I think, whereas sentences such as (15) and (19) are better represented by a structure such as(17):

17.

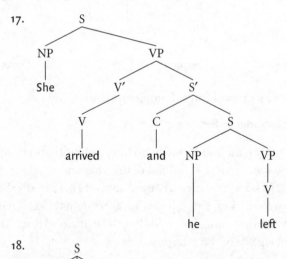

18.

```
        S
      / | \
     S and S
```

19. Jane Austen, *Emma*, Vol 1, chap 1
    You made a lucky guess; and that is all that can be said.

I leave it to the reader to decide whether (17) or (18) is more appropriate for (15), (16), and (19) and others like them (see Chapter 3, Section 4, for more arguments).

5. Terminological labyrinth

In this short section, I will list some synonyms or near synonyms for terms related to clauses that are in use in the grammatical tradition. Remember, in this book, clause and sentence are used interchangeably:

20. sentence = main clause = independent clause = superordinate clause = S
21. clause = embedded clause = embedded sentence = dependent clause
    = subordinate clause
22. complementizer = subordinating conjunction = C
23. coordinator = coordinating conjunction

Also note that a main clause always has to be finite, but an embedded clause can be finite or non-finite.

6. Conclusion

This chapter discusses sentences that contain more than one lexical verb. When that occurs, there is a main clause (or sentence) and one or more subordinate clauses (or embedded sentences). The latter clauses can be represented as S's consisting of a complementizer and a clause. Each subordinate clause has a function in the sentence (or in that phrase, see Chapter 10). Examples of all the functions that clauses fulfill are given. Two structures for coordinated sentences are given and the reader is invited to choose for him- or herself. Key terms are **clause and sentence; main clause and subordinate; S′, S, and C; complementizer; coordinator.**

Exercises:

A. Draw trees for:

24. Zelda noticed that candies disappear.
25. They suggested that the sketch was done by daughters of the architect.
26. They fussed that the main computer was down again.
27. They purified books because they didn't like them.
28. I heard that a manuscript has been stolen.
29. Amir didn't know if Zoya was unhappy.

30. He left the party because she arrived.
31. Fortunately, Zelda discovered that Zoltan hated her.
32. Because the snow was bad, the traffic on that street became impossible.
33. Zoltan mentioned that Bela had gone to the library without his rain jacket.
34. That two paintings were stolen from the Met is false.
35. I wondered whether that would happen.

B. List the functions of the embedded clauses in (24) to (35).

Advanced problems

C. Draw trees for (36) and (37). The latter is a non-finite and will be discussed in the next chapter:

36. I wonder what he saw.
37. He told us where to go.

D. There are a few special types of sentences that we haven't had a chance to talk about above, namely (38) and (39):

38. If he was rich, (then) he would own an island.
39. He did that task as well as he could.

We won't draw trees for these, but think about the structures. They are very different from each other.

Class discussion

D. Sentences such as *I mentioned that Sue won the Nobel Prize yesterday* are ambiguous. How are they (draw trees) and how would you change them if you wanted to avoid ambiguity?

Keys to the Exercises

The tree for (24) is:

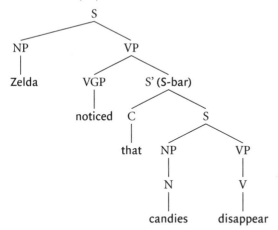

For (25):

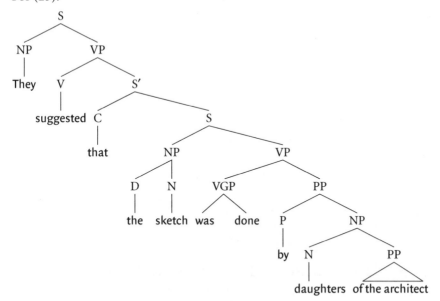

For (26):

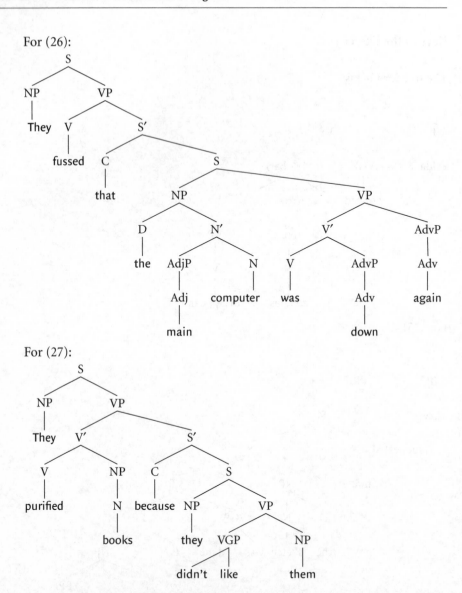

For (27):

Sentence (28) involves an embedded object and is similar in structure to (24), (25), and (26). Sentence (29) is similar too, except that *if* is in the C. Sentence (30) has the same structure as (27). The structure for (31) is:

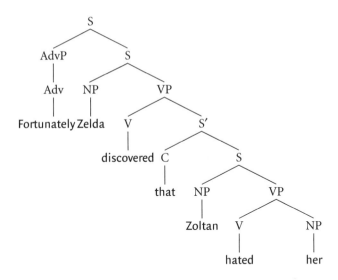

The structure for (32) is as below. I have drawn this slightly differently with the words at the bottom in a straight line. See what you like best:

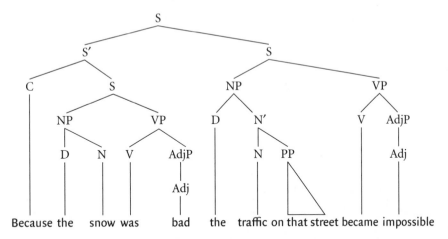

Sentence (33) is similar to the above embedded objects, and so is (35), except that *whether* is in C. The structure of (34) is as below, with the embedded clause as subject:

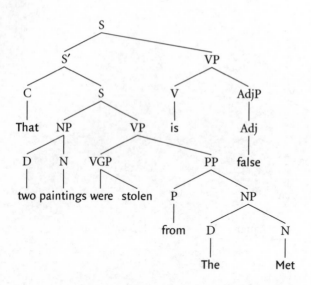

B. In (24), (25), (26), (28), (29), (31), (33), and (35) it is a Direct Object; in (27), (30), and (32) an Adverbial; and in (34), it is a Subject.

C.

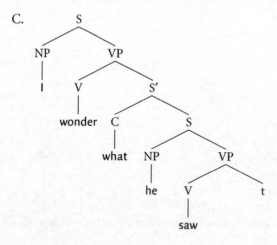

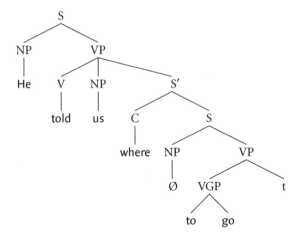

D. In (38), the two clauses are not coordinated since the *if*-clause is subordinate to the other. In (39), *as well as he could* is an adverbial, and one could argue that the head is the adverb *well*, so that it is an AdvP in form. The head *well* is modified by a clause *as he could* that is dependent on the adverb *as*. This is quite a complex construction.

Special topic: Preposition or complementizer: the 'preposition' *like*

Especially since the 1980s, *like* has expanded its uses tremendously. It is sometimes claimed that it is the most frequent word in the speech of certain groups of speakers (see cartoon below). Prescriptive grammarians are not too pleased with this development, but tend to focus on the use of *like* as a complementizer.

The prescriptive rule goes as follows: "*like* is a preposition and not a complementizer. This means that it can introduce an NP but not a clause. Instead of *like*, *as* is used to introduce a sentence".

Fowler (1926 [1950]: 325ff.) is not too clear in the following excerpt but is not happy with the use of *like* except as preposition. He writes:

> It will be best to dispose first of what is, if it is a misuse at all, the most flagrant & easily recognizable misuse of *like*. A sentence from Darwin quoted in the OED [Oxford English Dictionary] contains it in a short & unmistakable form: *Unfortunately few have observed like you have done.* Every illiterate person uses this construction daily; it is the established way of putting the thing

among all who have not been taught to avoid it ... in good writing this particular *like* is very rare.

Swan (1980: 73) is more low-key and says that "[i]n informal American English, *like* is very often used as a conjunction instead of *as*".

According to prescriptive authorities, we should allow *like* as a preposition, as in (40), but not as a complementizer, as in (41) to (47):

40. Certainly, he is not like Mr. Knightley.
    (Jane Austen, *Emma*, Vol 1, chap 4)
41. Shop like you mean it. (advertizement)
42. Eat it as it is, right out of the pouch. Enjoy it like today's astronauts do. (on a package of space food)
43. "People have never been down and out like they are today", said Angela Alioto, a candidate for Mayor... (NYT, 26 Aug 1991)
44. "We just felt like this year we needed to get away for a while" (NYT, 10 Aug 1991)
45. I felt like I could tell you anything. Now I don't feel like I can anymore. (quoted in Tannen's *That's not what I meant*).
46. Winston tastes good like a cigarette should. What do you want: Good grammar or good taste? (an ad in the 1960s)
47. Beach Boys' Song
    She forgot all about the library like she told her old man now.

Except as complementizer and preposition, *like* is often used to mark direct speech, as in (48), focus, as in (49), or to soften a request or demand, as in (50). These uses are not accepted in formal speech either, even though some are old, as (51) and (52) show, quoted in the OED:

48. ... So the other girl goes like: 'Getting an autograph is like, be brave and ask for it'. So I got it. I just went up to him and he like. 'O.K ...
49. I couldn't get to class because, well, like I had this accident on the freeway.
50. Tiffany, you, like, still owe me that $10.
51. Dunbar Poems, xix, 19
    3on man is lyke out of his mynd
52. Spenser, *Fairie Queen*, iv, x, 56
    all looking on, and like atonisht staring

As a speaker of English, when would you use the *like* of (41) and when the *like* of (48) to (52)?

REAL LIFE ADVENTURES by Gary Wise and Lance Aldrich

Why no one diagrams sentences anymore.

8   Non-finite clauses

Chapter 7 deals with finite embedded sentences, i.e. those sentences that contain finite verbs. The present chapter deals with non-finite sentences (or clauses), i.e. those that contain only non-finite verbs. Non-finite sentences can only function as parts of another sentence; they are not considered well-formed sentences on their own in formal writing but as sentence fragments.

First, I list the three kinds of non-finite clauses and a review of the characteristics of non-finites. Then, as in the case of finite embedded sentences, I will illustrate the functions that non-finite clauses have. Tree structures are provided in Section 3, and instances of coordinated non-finites in Section 4.

1.   Non-finite clauses

There are three kinds of non-finite clauses, namely those whose verb groups contain infinitives, or present participles, or past participles. We'll first consider infinitives.

There are two types of infinitives: one with *to*, as in (1), and a bare one, without *to*, as in (2). The bare one occurs only after verbs such as *make, see, hear* and *feel*, but the *to*-infinitive occurs very frequently:

1. I expected him **to go.**
2. I made him **leave.**

Apart from infinitives, there are two other kinds of non-finite Verb Groups, usually referred to as participles: a present participle ending in *-ing*, as in (3), and a past participle ending in *-ed* or *-en*, as in (4):

3. **Walking** down Rural Road, he was bothered by the traffic lights.
4. **Arrested** last night, he is in jail this morning.

The form of *arrested* is a regular past participle because it ends in *-ed*. Remember, however, that past participles, like simple past tenses, can have irregular endings.

As mentioned in Chapter 6, non-finites fail to express tense. Thus in (5), the non-finite *to walk* in the subordinate clause is neither past nor present, but the finite verb *is/was* in the main clause determines the tense:

5.   [To walk in the Superstitions] is/was nice.

In addition, the verb in non-finite clauses displays no person or number marking, as is shown by the ungrammaticality of *walks* in (6):

6.   *[For him to walks in the Superstitions] is nice.

A third characteristic of non-finites is that the subject is not nominative. Thus, (7), (8), and (9) are grammatical with accusative *him*, but (10) with nominative *he* is not:

7.   I want [him to go].
8.   I heard [him/Edward playing a song].
9.   She couldn't bear to see [him/Edward suffering].
10. *I want he to go.

The non-finite clause can also be replaced by a verbal noun, as in (11), and then the subject bears genitive case, namely *his/Edward's*, rather than accusative or objective, as in (7), (8), and (9). This construction is often called a gerund in traditional grammars, and *suffering* is a noun rather than a verb:

11. She couldn't bear to see [his/Edward's suffering].

As (12) shows, a non-finite clause by itself is not a complete sentence:

12. *Him to go.

2.   The functions of non-finites

The functions of non-finite clauses are similar to those of finite ones. They function at sentence level as subject in (13), and (5) above; direct object in (14), and (7) above; adverbial in (15), and (3) and (4) above; and subject predicate in (16):

13. [Eating pancakes] is a pleasant thing.
14. I love [eating pancakes].

15. He went there [to see them].

16. The problem is [to decide on what to eat].

In Chapter 10, non-finite clauses will be shown to function inside phrases as well. Here too, their function is similar to that of finite clauses.

3. The structure: S'?

The structure for non-finites is debatable. I represent it by means of an S', as in (17), the structure for (7):

17.

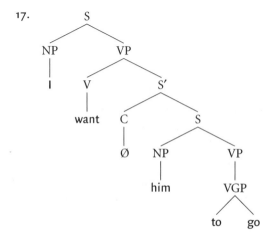

This means that I assume an empty complementizer which can be filled by *for* in a number of cases such as (18):

18. I want for you to do your homework.

Non-finite clauses need not include a subject. The subject may be understood, as in (19). However, rather than represent the infinitive by just a VP, I will use an S', with an empty C and an empty subject NP, as in (20):

19. To hike around Weaver's Needle is pleasant.

20.

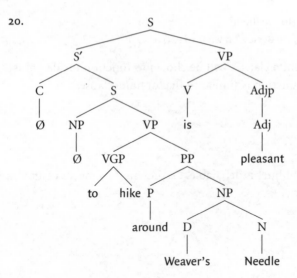

The reason I prefer (20) is that it is pleasant for **someone** to walk around Weaver's Needle; the tree expresses that there is a subject even if this subject is left unidentified. To indicate that the PP is an adverbial, you could make it a sister to V'.

Sentences such as (3) and (4) above can also be represented as S', as in (21) and (22). However, as in the case of infinitives, there are grammarians who prefer a structure with fewer empty positions, i.e. a VP rather than an S':

21.

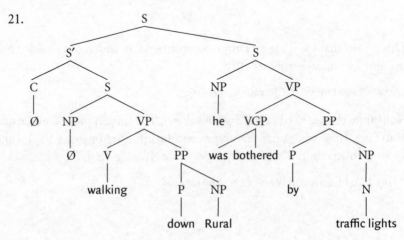

22.

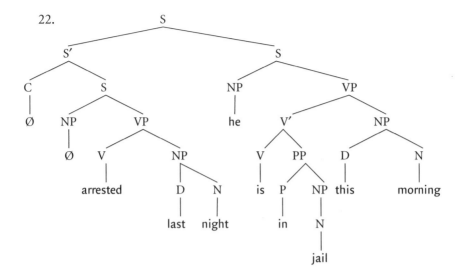

4. Coordinating non-finites

As is the case with finite clauses, non-finite clauses can be coordinated, as in (23), where the coordinated present participles function as subject:

23. Gossiping about Zelda and chewing gum is hard to do at the same time.

Other examples are given in (24) to (26). The coordinated non-finites in (24) are the object to *think*; in (25) the complement to *inclination* (this will get clearer in Chapter 10); and in (26), there are three coordinate clauses functioning as subject predicate. We can go over these in class, but the basic structure is like other coordinates, namely as in (27), a simplified (24):

24. She could not think of Emma losing a single pleasure, or suffering an hour's ennui (adapted from *Emma*)
25. *Emma*, Vol 2, chap 6
    But Emma, in her own mind, determined that he did not know what he was talking about, and that he shewed a very amiable inclination to settle early in life, and to marry.
26. The aim of this course is to understand some of the complexities of language, to use syntactic arguments, and to create some tolerance for different varieties of English.

27.

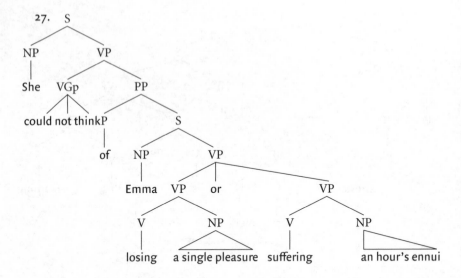

Note that, for practical reasons (the tree not fitting on the page), I am using a coathanger in (27).

5. Conclusion

In this chapter, non-finite clauses are discussed. Their structure and function is quite similar to that of finite clauses. The difference in terms of structure is that often the complementizer does not appear and the subject can be absent. Non-finites function at sentence level as subjects, direct objects, adverbials, and subject predicates. Key terms are **non-finite Verb Groups, namely infinitives, bare infinitives, present participle, past participle** and **empty subjects.**

Exercises

A.   Draw trees for the following sentences:

28.   Drawing trees is easy.
29.   Emma wanted to do that.
30.   For Ed to be resigning from that job is stupid.
31.   Anselm made Vicky read the paper.
32.   I saw turkeys crossing the street.
33.   Santa set the alarm to be on time.

B. Construct a sentence with two embedded sentences, one of which must be a non-finite clause functioning as direct object.

C. Construct a sentence with three non-finite clauses.

Class discussion

D. The following sentences are ambiguous. Why?

34. Flying planes can be dangerous.
35. Visiting aliens should be amusing on a Monday morning.

E. Read Keats' poem "To Autumn" and list the finite verbs. Discuss the difference between the first two stanzas in class.

> To Autumn
>
> Season of mists and mellow fruitfulness,
> Close bosom friend of the maturing sun,
> Conspiring with him how to load and bless
> With fruit the vines that round the thatch-eaves run;
> To bend with apples the mossed cottage-trees,
> And fill all fruit with ripeness to the core;
> To swell the gourd, and plump the hazel shells
> With a sweet kernel; to set budding more,
> And still more, later flowers for the bees,
> Until they think warm days will never cease,
> For summer has o'er-brimmed their clammy cells.
>
> Who hath not seen thee oft amid thy store?
> Sometimes whoever seeks abroad may find
> Thee sitting careless on a granary floor,
> Thy hair soft-lifted by the winnowing wind;
> Or on a half-reaped furrow sound asleep,
> Drowsed with the fume of poppies, while thy hook
> Spares the next swath and all its twined flowers:
> And sometimes like a gleaner thou dost keep
> Steady thy laden head across a brook;
> Or by a cider-press, with patient look,
> Thou watchest the last oozings hours by hours.

Where are the songs of spring? Ay, where are they?
Think not of them, thou hast thy music too, —
While barred clouds bloom the soft-dying day,
And touch the stubble-plains with rosy hue;
Then in a wailful choir the small gnats mourn
Among the river sallows, borne aloft
Or sinking as the light wind lives or dies;
And full-grown lambs loud bleat from hilly bourn;
Hedge-crickets sing; and now with treble soft
The red-breast whistles from a garden-croft;
And gathering swallows twitter in the skies.

Keys to the Exercises

A.   For (28), using 'empties', the tree would be:

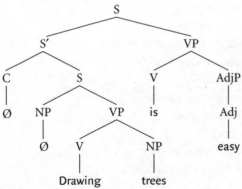

For (29), it is:

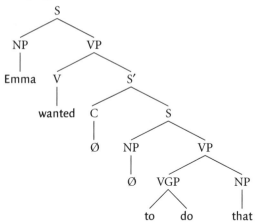

For (30):

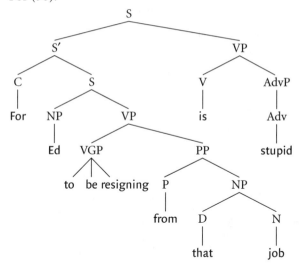

For (31):

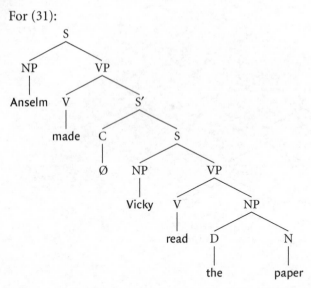

Sentence (32) has the same structure as (31). A structure for (33) is:

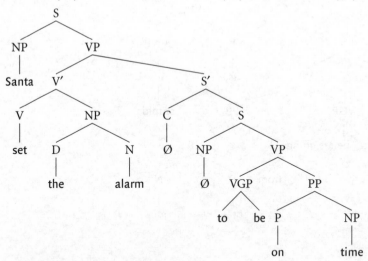

B. Kim and Paul hoped [to see unicorns in the parking lot] [because they had studied their habits].

C. I intend [to see if [looking out the window more often] means [working better]].

Special topic: Dangling or misplaced modifiers, or improper adverbials

The prescriptive rule is as follows: "The subject of a clause with a participle in it (i.e. without a subject of its own) must be the same as the subject of the main clause".

Swan (1980:455) provides the following rule: "It is usually considered [note the qualifiers, EvG] a mistake to make sentences like these in which the subjects are different: *Looking out of the window of our hotel, there were lots of mountains …* However, there are some very common expressions which break this rule. *Generally speaking, … Judging from his expression, … Considering, …*". Fowler (1926 [1950]:675) says that "it is to be remembered that there is a continual change going on by which certain participles or adjectives acquire the character of prepositions or adverbs, no longer needing the prop of a noun to cling to". Hence, neither Swan nor Fowler are very critical of the use.

'Incorrect' uses are given in (36) to (39). Some of these are funny because we automatically think of the modifiers as having the same subject as the main clause:

36. Running down the street, the house was on fire.
37. Referring to your letter of 5 September, you do not state …
38. Reading your essays last night, there were many good examples of dangling modifiers.
39. Although spoken in Shakespeare's First Folio, we do not speak that way today.
40. Lying in a heap on the floor, she found the clothes.

Sometimes, they seem to be able to refer to either the subject or the closest NP, as in (41), or to neither. The first meaning we come up with in (41) is the one where the waiter is drenched in syrup:

41. The waiter brought the waffles to the table drenched in maple syrup.

The original subtitle of the book, adapted from Hamlet, was (42). After quite a bit of feedback, mainly from students, I decided against having it as a subtitle. It is, however, also an instance of a possibly misplaced modifier. It depends on who is sleeping:

42. Sleeping in mine orchard, a serpent stung me.

Review of Chapters 7 and 8

Chapters 7 and 8 deal with embedded sentences. If a sentence contains more than one lexical verb, it contains multiple sentences (also called clauses). The structure of the embedded sentence is an S′ which accommodates the complementizer and the S. The structure of coordinate sentences is discussed as well.

Answers will be provided for the review questions, but not for the sample exam covering these chapters.

Exercises

A. In the following sentences, please identify the finite and non-finite clauses that function as subjects, direct objects, subject predicates, and adverbials.

1. Some linguistic historians prefer to believe that languages live and die by social evolution.
2. They saw him cross the street without looking.
3. It is gratifying to see that idea becoming more accepted.
4. Since the advent of printing, the standard language may have developed that way because of increased standardization.
5. The president that founded this organization was arrested twice before he was replaced.

B. Which are the lexical verbs in (1) to (5) and which are the finite Verb Groups (i.e. a VGP containing a finite verb)?

Keys to the exercises

A. 1. Some linguistic historians prefer [OBJECT: to believe [OBJECT: that languages live and die by social evolution]].
   2. They saw [OBJECT: him cross the street [ADVERBIAL: without looking]].
   3. It is gratifying [SUBJECT: to see [OBJECT: that idea becoming more accepted]. See Chapter 7 for extraposed subjects.
   4. Since the advent of printing, the standard language may have developed that way because of increased standardization. NONE
   5. The president that founded this organization was arrested twice [ADVERBIAL: before he was replaced]. Note that this sentence also contains a relative clause. Relative clauses modify an N and do not function independently. For more on this, see Chapter 10.

B. In (1), *prefer, believe, live, die* are lexical. In (2), *saw, cross,* and *looking* are; in (3) *is, see, becoming;* in (4), *developed;* in (5), *founded, arrested, replaced* are. Finite VGPs in (1) are *prefer, live* and *die;* in (2), *saw;* in (3), *is;* in (4), *may have developed;* and in (5), *founded, was arrested, was replaced.*

Exam, covering Chapters 7 and 8

1. What is prescriptively wrong with sentence (a)? Give the name of this phenomenon and explain why it is wrong.
   a. Although spoken by Shakespeare, we don't speak that way today.

2. Identify the (main and subordinate) clauses by means of brackets in the sentences below. Indicate which clauses are finite:

   The future of 100,000 refugees was dealt another blow this week after the Bhutanese government rejected a UN formula. Bhutan and Nepal started negotiations to solve the problem of the people in refugee camps in 1992. Since then many high-level meetings have taken place without resulting in a solution, however.

3. Draw trees for (b), (c), and (d):
   b. To be or not to be will be decided tomorrow.
   c. Those Martians decided that they would take along some dogs on their trip.
   d. They wanted to see him very much before leaving Phoenix.

9 The structure of the NP, AdjP, AdvP, and PP

Up to now, we have mainly seen phrases function at sentence level (as subjects, direct objects, subject predicates, adverbials, etc.). In this chapter, some examples are given in which phrases function inside other phrases, as modifiers to the heads of these phrases.

Grammatical categories such as the determiner also function inside phrases, whereas auxiliaries function in the Verb Group, see Chapter 6, and complementizers link one sentence to another. The grammatical categories only function inside other phrases: they never function as subjects or objects, i.e. at sentence level.

Some of the structure of the NP, AdjP, AdvP, and PP has already been provided in Chapter 3. The present chapter elaborates on the functions of the different parts of these phrases. The functions are determiner, modifier, head, and complement. The main difference between functions inside a VP (see Chapters 4 and 5) and those inside an NP, PP, AdvP, and AdjP is that the direct and indirect object, subject and object predicate in the VP correspond to the complement in the other phrases. The adverbial in the VP corresponds to the modifier in the other phrases. Thus, in the NP, PP, AdjP, and AdvP, the functions are not as diverse as in the VP, and of two kinds only, namely complement and modifier. Often, these are not distinguished in the tree structure. Another point to notice is that complements to AdjPs and NPs are optional, whereas they aren't in the case of VPs.

1. The structure and function of AdjP, AdvP, and PP

Instances of complex Adjective Phrases are *blatantly illegal* in (1), *perfectly safe, very nice, really interesting, too good.*

1. Dumping garbage on the street is [blatantly illegal].

They are called AdjPs because their heads are adjectives, i.e. *illegal* in (1). A structure for an AdjP would be as in (3), where *illegal* is the head and the adverb *blatantly* modifies it. The adverb expresses the manner of the illegality and is comparable to an adverbial in the VP, as in (2). Traditionally, the adverbial inside an AdjP, as in (1), or inside an NP is called modifier, rather than adverbial inside the VP, as in (2):

2. He blatantly defied the authorities.

3.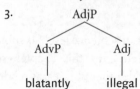

So far, the AdjP and AdvP have contained heads and modifiers. However, as in the case of VPs (and NPs, see the next section), there can be a complement to the adjective as well (not to the adverb though). For instance, in (4), *of his catch* does not describe the manner or the place of being proud but what someone is proud of, i.e. *of his catch* is the complement of *proud* (inside the VP we'd call it a direct object). The same is true of *that waste* in (5):

4. He was blatantly proud of his catch.
5. There is something that is very illegal about that waste.

A tree for the AdjP in (5) is as in (6):

6.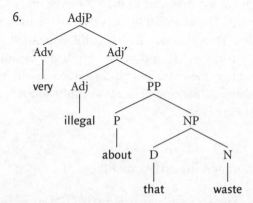

As in the case of VPs where objects are sisters to V, the complement *about that waste* is sister to the Adjective. In (6), I have put in the (intermediate) label Adj' (pronounced 'Adj-bar'). In Chapters 3 and 5, we mentioned this intermediate node in connection with the NP and the VP. Some other examples of adjectives that have complements are *able, afraid, aware, conscious, fond, glad, happy, mad, proud, reasonable,* and *successful.*

AdjPs typically only have modifiers preceding the head (except for a few, e.g. *enough,* that come after), unlike NPs as will be shown in the next section. Their complements do follow the head though and are generally optional. Thus, (4) is the maximal structure of the AdjP, with the functions listed in (7):

7. | Modifier | Head | Complement |
    |----------|------|------------|
    | AdvP | Adj | PP |
    | blatantly | proud | of his catch |

As we'll see in the next chapter, the complement can also be a full sentence or clause.

Adverbs have no complements, as shown by the ungrammatical (8), and their typical structure is one with a modifier that precedes the head, e.g. *very* in *very illegally*:

8. *He dumped waste illegally about it.

The adverbs that modify adverbs are few in number. Some examples are *very, so, too, extremely, really* (or *real,* see special topic to Chapter 2), and *quite.*

The structure of the PP is relatively straightforward, with a head and an NP complement, as in (6) above. The preposition is the head of the PP and an NP always functions as complement. There are a limited number of modifiers to PPs, e.g. *right* and *straight,* as in *he went right to school.*

2. The structure of the NP and functions inside it

Typical instances of NPs would be (9a) and (9b):

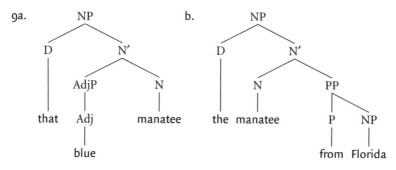

The functions of the different elements inside an NP are determiner, modifier, complement, and head. In (9a), the AdjP *blue* modifies the head (it describes a quality) and the determiner *that* points to a particular *manatee*. There is no complement. Because *blue* precedes the head, it is sometimes called the pre-modifier. *From Florida* in (9b) modifies the head (tells you where from), but follows the head and is therefore sometimes called the postmodifier.

An NP in English can also contain what is called a complement to the noun. Unlike objects in the VP, complements to N and Adj are optional. For instance, in (10) to (13), a number of NPs is listed, with the complement in brackets. Sentence (11) skips ahead to the next chapter since the complement is a finite clause:

10. The teacher [of Martian]
11. The story [that Arafat met Clinton was reported widely]
12. The student [of chemistry]
13. The discussion [about welfare]

Because both complements and modifiers are optional, it is sometimes hard to distinguish. One way that may help is that if you change the nouns in (10) to (13) to verbs (hard to do with (11)), the complements become direct objects:

14. You teach Martian.
15. He narrated that Arafat had met Clinton.
16. She studied chemistry.
17. They discussed welfare.

As in the case of objects inside the VP (Chapter 4), AdjP and PP (previous section), complements to the N can be represented in the tree as sisters to the head, in this case N, as in (18) and (19). We'll come back to (19) in the next chapter:

18.

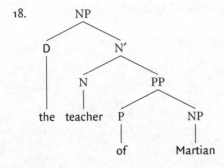

19.

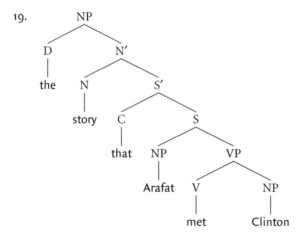

So far, we have seen that the elements of an NP in English function as determiner, head, modifier, and complement. This is summarized in (20) (the '∧'
indicates that there can be more than one). The name (i.e. label or realization)
of each of these functions is listed underneath:

20. determiner modifierˆ head   complement   modifierˆ
    D   AdjPˆ   N   PP   PPˆ
    the   nice   student of chemistry from Macedonia

In tree form, (20) looks like (21), with the modifier expanded:

21.

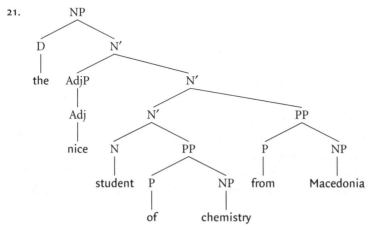

As you may remember from Chapter 2, the pre-determiner may be added as a
function inside the NP. In (22), three quantifiers that function in this way are
given. In a tree, they would precede the D, but I won't go into this here:

22.   All the nice books; half the people; both my pictures.

The determiner is special in that it is both a category name, which includes articles, quantifiers, demonstratives, possessives, etc. (see Chapter 2), as well as a function name.

The last element we are adding to the NP is the focusser or emphasizer. Some of the ones that occur in English are *just, only, especially,* and *even,* as in (23). Most of these are tricky in that they can be used in other ways too, e.g. *even* and *just* are also adjectives, and most are adverbs as well:

23.   George Berkeley, *Principles* 97
      then it will perhaps gravel even a philosopher to comprehend it.

3.   Arguments for distinguishing complements from modifiers

As I mentioned in Section 2, inside the NP, some elements are more closely related to the head N than others. Many grammarians refer to these as complements and modifiers respectively. They can be compared to the objects (even though the latter are more obligatory) and the adverbials in the VP. In this section, I provide some arguments for distinguishing complement from modifier with trees that show the distinction. In general, grammarians do not distinguish these two carefully in the NP, see e.g. (37), (39), (40), and (41) below.

3.1 Complement and modifier follow the head N

In the tree structure, one can find out the difference between the complement and the modifier by looking at which element is sister to which one. For instance, in (24) *of physics* is sister to N and is therefore the complement, whereas *from England* is not a sister to N and is therefore the modifier. There can only be one complement but many modifiers and the order between complement and modifier cannot be reversed as (25) shows. This is the first argument you can use to distinguish between complements and modifiers:

24.

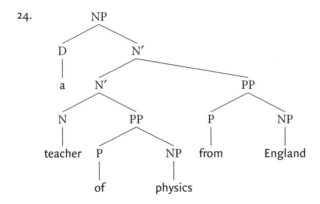

25. *A teacher from England of physics.

Apart from word order, there is a second way to distinguish complements from modifiers and it involves determining what pronoun one can use to pronominalize certain parts of the NP. In (24), *teacher of physics* and *teacher of physics from England* are N's. There is an argument that the status of N' is different from that of N and NP. It can be shown that the N' can be replaced by *one*, but that the N cannot be replaced by *one*. In (26), *one* replaces *teacher of physics*, i.e. an N', and the sentence is grammatical; in (27), *one* replaces *teacher*, i.e. an N, and this results in an ungrammatical sentence:

26. I know the teacher of physics from England and the one from France.
27. *I know the teacher of physics from England and the one of chemistry.

Hence, the first piece of evidence for distinguishing complement and modifier is that the complement is closer to the head, as in (24). Secondly, there is also evidence for the special status of the intermediate category N' in that it can be replaced by *one*.

A third test for distinguishing complements from modifiers is coordination. It is possible to coordinate two complements, as in (28), or two modifiers, as in (29), but not a complement and a modifier, as in (30):

28. The teachers of physics and of chemistry.
29. The teachers from Turkey and from Spain.
30.*The teachers from Turkey and of physics.

3.2 Complement and modifier precede the head N

Complements and modifiers can also precede the N, as in (31). Again the complement is closer to the head than the modifier. Their order cannot be reversed, as (32) shows, and there can only be one complement but many modifiers, as in (33):

31.

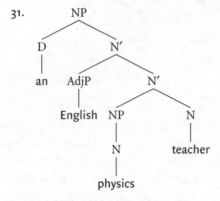

32. *A physics English teacher.

33. A nice, patient, English chemistry teacher.

I have shown that there is evidence that complements and modifiers are distinguished in an NP: their order, coordination, and pronominalization differ.

4. Conclusion

In this chapter, I have discussed the different functions of elements in the AdjP, AdvP, PP, and NP. These functions are similar to the ones in the VP, discussed in Chapters 4 and 5, with the exception of the names given and their optionality. Thus, the adverbial of the VP is called modifier in the AdjP, AdvP and NP, and the different kinds of objects in the VP are not differentiated and just called complements in the AdjP, PP, and NP. The NP may also contain a determiner where the VP has a subject. The complements in the NP and AdjP are usually optional, whereas objects and predicates in the VP are obligatory. Key terms in Sections 1 and 2 are **determiner, modifier, head, complement**; in Section 3, they are **complement as opposed to modifier; word order; pronominalization; and coordination.**

Exercises

A. Provide a tree structure for the following NPs (use NP, AdjP, D, etc.). Also
    list the functions of the different elements.

    34. one of their irrational responses
    35. the reaction to the environmental study of this area
    36. a hilarious look at two geniuses
    37. four fluffy feathers on a Fiffer-feffer-feff (from Dr. Seuss's ABC)

B. Provide a tree structure for the following sentences:

    38. This wonderful fridge is banned in Montana.
    39. A very curious red book with ink stains was found.
    40. He hides behind the pile of books on his desk.
    41. The lovely pig from Wyoming told the bureaucrat in Washington the story of
         his life.

C. In the sentences below, adapted from *The Death of Ivan Ilych* by Leo
    Tolstoy, find the PPs that function as modifiers inside phrases:

    42. During an interval in the Melvinski trial, the members and public prosecu-
         tor met in Ivan Egorovich Shebek's private room, where the conversation
         turned on the celebrated Krasovski case.
    43. On receiving the news of Ivan Ilych's death, the first thought of each of the
         gentlemen in that private room was of the changes and promotions it might
         occasion among themselves or their acquaintances.
    44. Leaning against the wall in the hall downstairs near the cloak-stand was a
         coffin-lid covered with cloth of gold, ornamented with gold cord and tassels.

Optional Exercises for Section 3

D. Try to draw trees for (45) and (46). Which PPs and NPs are complements?
    Provide reasons for your answer:

    45. Canadian students of English
    46. a French Old English student.

Class discussion

E. The first sentence of the text in C is actually as in (47). Do you think there is ambiguity? Is the *trial* postmodified by the PP that follows, or is that PP an independent adverbial?

47. During an interval in the Melvinski trial in the large building of the Law Courts the members and public prosecutor met in Ivan Egorovich Shebek's private room, where the conversation turned on the celebrated Krasovski case.

F. Compare the NP in (48) with the S in (49). What are the similiarities/ differences?

48. Stella's destruction of that awful set of dishes.
49. Stella destroyed that awful set of dishes.

G. Discuss how sentences such as (50) and (51) are ambiguous, and how you might draw trees disambiguating them:

50. A chocolate toy factory.
51. A Belgian chocolate factory.

Keys to the Exercises

A. The structure for (34) is as follows, with *one* as the head and *of their irrational responses* as the modifier. In this phrase, the determiner *one* is functioning as noun head (see Chapter 2 for other determiners that do this). A test for picking the head is making the phrase into a subject and then checking the agreement on the verb (*One of their responses was to …* and not *One of their responses were…*):

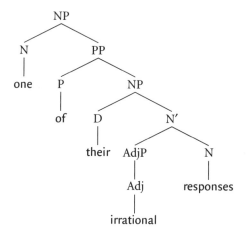

In (35), *the* is the determiner, *reaction* the head, and the rest is the complement. Notice that each NP inside the complement could be analyzed too, but we won't do that here:

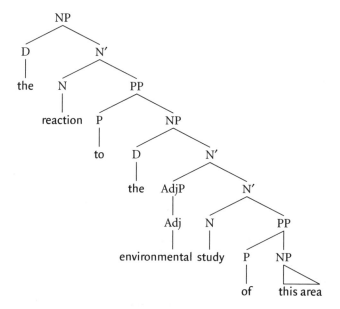

In (36), *a* is the determiner, *hilarious* the modifier, *look* the head, and the PP the complement:

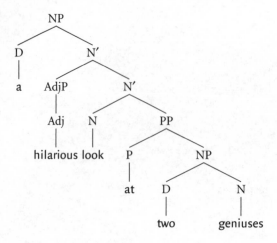

In (37), *four* is the determiner, *fluffy* is the modifier, *feathers* the head, and the PP is the (post-)modifier (to indicate this, the PP could be sister to N′):

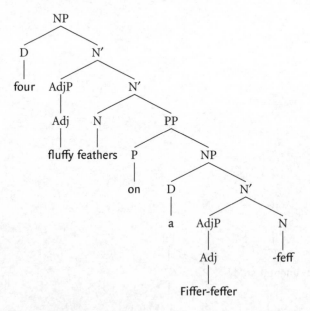

B. Many people will draw (38) as in (a). However, you could make the PP *in Montana* sister to V′ to express that it is an adverbial, as in (b):

a.

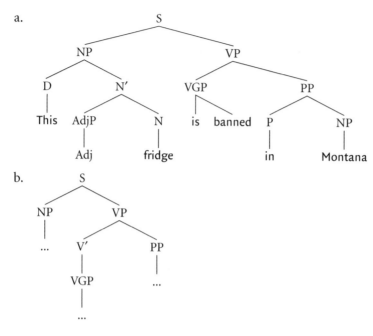

b.

A possible tree for (39) is:

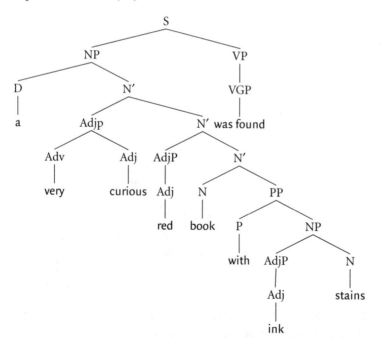

There are other correct trees for (39). You could put *red* and *book* more closely together than *book* and the PP, as I've done above. Also, if you wanted to express that the PP in (39) is a modifier not a complement, you could make it sister to N′ rather than N, as in:

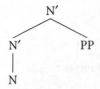

A structure for (40) is as follows. There are again other possible trees for (40), e.g. as in (39), one could indicate that the PPs are modifiers by making them sisters to N′. Notice in (40) that *on my desk* is modifying *a pile of books* but I have left that out of the tree. If it were an independent adverbial, it would mean that he hides on his desk behind a pile of books:

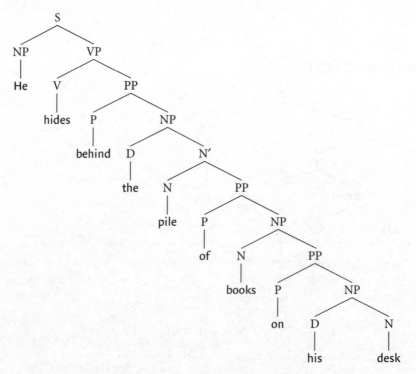

A tree as in (41) is a challenge if you don't have enough space. Doing it by hand will save you a lot of time over drawing it using a computer:

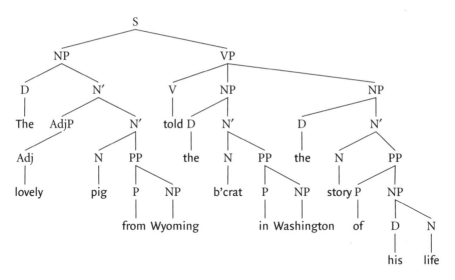

C. For (42): During an interval [in the Melvinski trial], the members and public prosecutor met in Ivan Egorovich Shebek's private room, where the conversation turned on the celebrated Krasovski case.

For (43): On receiving the news [of Ivan Ilych's death], the first thought [of each [of the gentlemen [in that private room]]] was of the changes and promotions it might occasion among themselves or their acquaintances.

For (44): Leaning against the wall [in the hall downstairs] near the cloak-stand was a coffin-lid covered with cloth [of gold], ornamented with gold cord and tassels.

Note that *with cloth of of gold* and *with gold and tassels* in (44) could in principle be postmodifiers to the adjective *covered* and *ornamented*. I analyze the latter as verbs in reduced relative clauses, and as a result the PPs are adverbials, not postmodifiers. *Near the cloak-stand* could be modifying *hall* if there were more than one hall. Since that seems unlikely, I analyze it as an adverbial. it could also modify *wall*.

D. The structure for (45) is as in (24) above, with *Canadian* as modifier and *of English* as complement. One of the reasons is that you can say *The Canadian one*, but not *the one of English*:

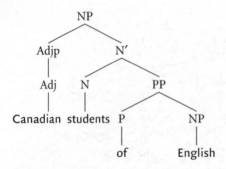

In (46), since *Old* is capitalized, it goes with *English*, and I have made it into a D, but modifier would be correct too. The modifier is *French* and the complement is *Old English*:

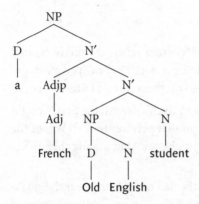

Special topic: Agreement

Rule: "The subject of a sentence (or to be more precise, the head of the phrase functioning as subject) agrees in person and number with the finite verb".

In Modern English, there is little agreement left on the verb. In standard English, apart from the verb *to be* (*I am, you are, s/he is, we are, you are,* and *they are* etc.), there is only a third person singular *-s* ending on verbs in the present tense (e.g. *I walk, you walk, s/he walks, we walk, you walk,* and *they walk*). In Old English, the endings were a lot more varied. Note that in some varieties of English, words such as *police* and *government* are singular, whereas in others, they are plural. In general, as long as you are consistent, either should be ok.

The difficulties usually occur with long subjects, as in (52) and (53), or with dummy subjects, as in (54). How could you change these?

52. One of the problems that they worried about continuously were solved rather quickly.
53. There are other things that you talked about that is not on the tape. (during the OJ trial)
54. There's some problems in syntax that they could not solve.

In earlier varieties of English, e.g. Shakespeare's English, there is much more agreement. For instance, in (55), the verb agrees with the second person singular *thou*. In some varieties of English, no agreement is left, as in (56), and in some, both singular and plural are possible, as in (57), from Hiberno-English:

55. Shakespeare, Julius Ceasar, I, 2, 18
    Caes. What **sayst** thou to me now? Speak once againe.
    Sooth. Beware the Ides of March.
56. The dog stay outside in the afternoon.
57. The boys **is/are** leaving.
    (from Henry 1995)

10 Clauses as parts of NPs, AdjPs, and PPs

In Chapters 7 and 8, the functions of finite and non-finite clauses are discussed at sentence level (e.g. as subjects or objects). The present chapter shows that clauses can also function inside the phrase as modifiers or complements. Traditionally, modifier clauses are called relative clauses and we'll continue that practice. I first show that PPs and AdvPs are different from NPs and AdjPs in that PPs and AdvPs do not generally allow clausal complements whereas NPs and AdjPs do. Then, examples and structures for complement and relative clauses inside the NP are given. Finally, examples of clausal complements to AdjPs are provided.

1. NPs and AdjPs as compared to PPs and AdvPs

Inside the NP or AdjP, clauses can often function as relatives (i.e. modifiers) or complements, as (1) and (2) show. These will be elaborated on in the next sections:

1. The man [who crossed Antarctica] was happy.
2. He was unsure [what he should say].

As shown in the previous chapter, AdvPs do not have complement or modifier PPs. They have no clausal complements or modifiers either. Prepositions have complement clauses such as in (3) but do not generally admit object clauses with a *that* complementizer, as (4) shows. Instead, a non-finite clause, as in (5), or a verbal noun, or gerund, as in (6) appears:

3. I relied on [what he wrote about clauses].
4. *I insisted on [that he/Stan should pay the bill].
5. I insisted on [him/Stan paying the bill].
6. I insisted on [his/Stan's paying (of) the bill].

Prepositions that express time, such as *before* or *after* as in (7), do introduce a clause but, as I mentioned in Chapter 7, they are then complementizers rather than prepositions:

7. He left [after she arrived].

2. NPs: Modifier (relative) and complement clauses

In the last chapter, I showed that, inside an NP, PPs function as either modifiers or as complements. Sentence (8), adapted from Chapter 9, contains both a PP complement (*of English*) and PP modifier (*from Macedonia*):

8. The student of English from Macedonia.

In this section, I show that clauses have the same two functions: complement in (9) and (10) or modifier in (11). When clauses function as modifiers, they are called relative clauses and are generally abbreviated as RC:

9. Reports [that he reached Mars] are exaggerated.
10. The fact [that he reached Mars] went unnoticed.
11. The stories [which he repeated often] are boring.

The bracketed S's in (9) and (10) are complements and therefore sisters to N, as shown for (9) in (12):

12.

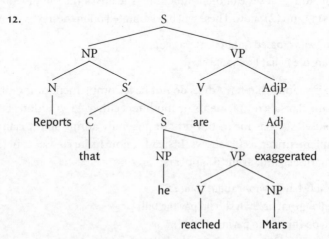

The S' in (9) and (10) is a complement for several reasons: (a) the N can be left out, as in (13) and (14), because the complement spells out what the stories and the fact are, (b) the head N *reports* plays no role inside the S', and (c) the complementizer has to be *that*. In (13), the agreement must of course be adjusted:

13. That he reached Mars is exaggerated.
14. That he reached Mars went unnoticed.

Clauses that modify NPs, such as the one in (11), are referred to as relative clauses because the noun they modify (*stories* in this case) plays a role (has a function) in the RC. The element that connects the noun and the clause, i.e. *who* in (15), is called a relative pronoun. In (11), the relative pronoun functions as the direct object of *repeat*. RCs are usually divided into restrictive as in (11) and non-restrictive (also called appositive), as in (15):

15. Clinton, who just returned from a trip to Cuba, intends to write a book.

Three differences between restrictive and non-restrictive relative clauses are listed in Table 10.1 but are discussed first. (a) Restrictive RCs can have a *that* as in (16), or a *who/which*, as in (11). In the non-restrictive RC (15), on the other hand, *that* is not possible, as (17) shows:

16. The stories that he told us often are boring.
17. *Clinton, that just returned from a trip to Cuba, intends to write a book.

(b) Restrictive RCs provide essential information. For instance, in (11), *the stories* is so general that the RC restricts and specifies the stories that are meant. In the case of (15), everyone living in the US at the beginning of the 21st century is expected to know who Clinton is and therefore the NP *Clinton* does not need to be restricted. The RC just provides background information that is not essential in knowing which noun is meant. (c) Since the information in non-restrictive RCs is background information, the non-restrictive RC in (15) can be surrounded by commas, and is therefore sometimes referred to as a parenthetical, whereas the restrictive RC in (16) cannot be.

Table 10.1. Restrictive and non-restrictive RCs

Restrictive	Non-Restrictive (or appositive)
a. WH or *that*	only WH
b. highly relevant information	additional information
c. commas cannot surround it	commas may surround it

The restrictive RC in (18) contrasts interestingly with a non-restrictive in (19). In (18), only a small set of climbers reached the top, but in (19), all the climbers did:

18. The hikers who reached the top were very tired.
19. The hikers, who reached the top, were very tired.

Some additional relative clauses are given in (20) to (22). Since they are all restrictive, both WH and *that* are possible, but they can also be left out, e.g. in (22):

20. The man about whom she heard that rumor is in prison.
21. The woman who(m)/that I heard this rumor about is pleasant.
22. The light (which/that) I just turned on is too bright.

There is a debate (see special topic at the end of this chapter) whether in (21) *who* should be used or *whom*. The same is true in (24) below. The reason is that when the function of the modified noun inside the RC is that of a prepositional object, as in (20) and (21), or direct object in (24), the accusative *whom* is preferred by prescriptive grammarians. In (15), (18), and (19) above, the noun plays the role of the subject and therefore only *who* is possible.

Structurally, the restrictive RC is said to be closer to the head but not as close as the complement in (12). The non-restrictive is often said to be sister to the NP, i.e. outside the NP. In Chapter 3 (Section 3), a number of structures were discussed that have a similar structure (with one NP branching to another), namely, coordinated NPs and appositive NPs. Many grammarians have noticed the similarities between non-restrictive RCs and appositive NPs, hence the alternative name of appositive RC. Thus, as mentioned, the appositive NP *We, the people of the United States, ...* could be rewritten as *We, who are the people of the United States, ...*

Structures of NPs with restrictive and non-restrictive RCs are given in (23) and (24) respectively. To indicate the function of the modified noun inside the RC, a t (short for trace) is introduced. For instance, in (23), *the woman* is being met, or the direct object in the RC, and a trace is placed as sister to the verb *met*. Similarly, in (24), *Zelda* is the object in the RC and a trace indicates that:

23. The woman that I met …

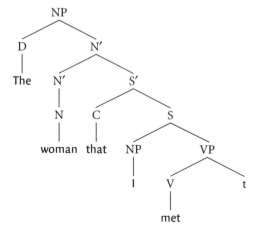

24. Zelda, who I know well, …

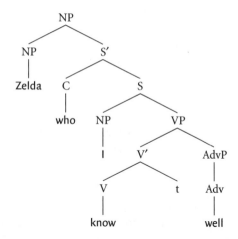

Note that I am focussing on trees in which the trace is an object since they are the least complex. In the (advanced) exercises, there will be other trees to draw.

Non-finite clauses, as in (25) to (27), just like their finite counterparts above, can be modifiers to N, as in (25) to (27):

25. The story [to tell him] is the following.
26. The story [written by him] is awful.
27. The author [writing those marvellous books] lives in Antarctica.

These non-finite clauses are sometimes called reduced relative clauses since one can paraphrase them with relative clauses. For instance, (25) to (27) are similar to the relative clause structures in (28) to (30):

28. The story [which you need to tell him] is the following.
29. The story [which was written by him] is awful.
30. The author [who is writing those marvellous books] lives in Antarctica.

We don't generally distinguish between restrictive and non-restrictive in these cases. Unlike finite clauses, non-finite clauses cannot be complements to nouns, as the ungrammatical (31) shows. Don't memorize this kind of information; just be able to analyze the structure of phrases:

31. *The story [for Arafat to have met Clinton] was untrue.

Thus, the functions of finite clauses inside the NP are complement and modifier. Modifiers are referred to as relative clauses (RCs) and can be restrictive or non-restrictive. Non-finite clauses only function as modifiers, and can be referred to as reduced relatives.

3. More on RCs

In this section, we'll briefly discuss a few other interesting facts about English RCs. First, we'll briefly look at relativized adverbials. Second, we'll look at prepositional and possessive relatives.

In Section 2, most examples have the relative occupying a subject position, e.g. (1) above, or an object position, e.g. (11) above. There is another frequently relativized function, namely that of adverbial, such as in (32) to (34):

32. The time when/that you should be here ...
33. The place where/that you should go ...
34. The reason why/that I avoided that party ...

The difference between subject, object, and adverbial relative is in the relative pronoun used. For subjects, *who* is used for humans, as in (1), (18), (19), and (24) above; *which* for non-humans, as in (28) and (29) above; and *that* for both if it is restrictive, as in (16). For (direct, indirect, and prepositional) objects, *whom* is used for humans in very formal English, *who* in less formal English; *which* for non-humans; and *that* in restrictive relatives for both. Certain varieties of English allow other options, e.g. *what* or *as*. Relativized adverbials as in (32) to (34), use the relative pronoun most appropriate, *when* for a time adverbial, *where* for place, etc.

In (20) and (21) above, RCs that relativize PPs occur. English has many options: it can 'strand' the preposition, as in (35), or 'pied pipe' it (as in the Rat Catcher of Hamelin), as in (36):

35. The translation which I insisted on was unavailable.
36. The translation on which I insisted was unavailable.

The relative pronoun can be left out, as in (37); and *that* can be used, but only when the preposition stays in place, as in (38):

37. The translation I insisted on.
38. The translation that I insisted on.

Possessives can be relativized too, as in (39), a sentence from an earlier chapter. They have an alternative as in (40), but the use of (39) is not restricted to human antecedents. Another set is given in (41) and (42):

39. You start with S, whose daughters are always NP and VP.
40. You start with S, the daughters of which are always NP and VP.
41. The book, whose author is well-known, was on NPR this morning.
42. The book, the author of which is well-known, was on NPR this morning.

4. AdjPs: Complement clauses

Finite and non-finite clauses, as in (43) to (45), can be complements to AdjPs:

43. He was unsure [what to do].
44. They were happy [that he went away].
45. He was proud [to have done it].

The structure of such AdjPs is as in (46) and (47). (Notice that in (46), the trace expresses that *what* is an object of the verb *do*):

46.

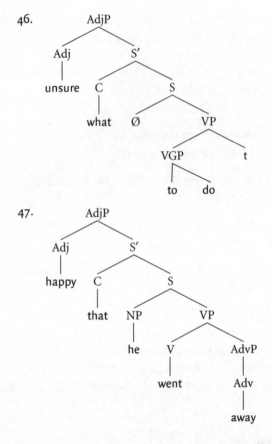

47.

Unlike nouns, adjectives only have complements; they do not have relative clauses (i.e. modifiers), but again this information is something you know automatically and need not memorize.

5. Conclusion

In this chapter, I have discussed finite and non-finite clauses functioning inside an NP or AdjP. Clauses have two functions: modifier and complement. Finite clauses that function as modifiers are called relative clauses, which can be divided in restrictive and non-restrictive relatives. Non-finite clauses functioning as modifiers are reduced relative clauses. In Chapters 7 and 8, functions of finite and non-finite clauses (at sentence level) were discussed, namely subject, direct object, adverbial and subject predicate. The key terms are **relative and** complement clauses; restrictive and non-restrictive relative clauses; and reduced relatives.

Exercises

A. Identify the clauses in (48) to (50). Are they complements or relatives; finite or non-finite?

48. The javelina that I saw next door was not afraid of coyotes.
49. The report that javelinas are dangerous is exaggerated.
50. Gerald, who lives next door, will be leaving soon.
51. The yellow fog that rubs its back upon the window-panes
    (from T. S.Eliot's *Love Song* for J. Alfred Prufock)
52. The president that founded this organization was arrested twice before he was replaced.

B. Draw trees for (48) to (52).

C. In the text below, identify the relative clauses. This is quite challenging:

> To educate as the practice of freedom is a way of teaching that anyone can learn. That learning process comes easiest to those of us who teach who also believe that there is an aspect of our vocation that is sacred; who believe that our work is not merely to share information but to share in the intellectual and spiritual growth of our students. To teach in a manner that respects and cares for the souls of our students is essential if we are to provide the necessary conditions where learning can most deeply and intimately begin.

> (from bell hooks *Teaching to Transgress*, 1994: 13)

D. Change one of the finite clauses in (52) into a non-finite one.

Class discussion

E. What is the basic structure of (53)? (Don't draw a tree!) Which are the relative clauses?

53. Shakespeare, *Loves Labour's Lost*, I, 2, 157
    Armado: I doe affect the very ground (which is base) where her shooe (which is baser) guided by her foote (which is basest) doth tread.

F. Can clauses ever be relatives or complements preceding the head? If yes, give examples. If no, give ungrammatical examples.

Keys to the Exercises

A. In (48), *that I saw next door* is a (restrictive) RC which is finite; in (49), *that javelinas are dangerous*, a finite complement; in (50), *who lives next door* is a (non-restrictive) RC which is finite; in (51), *that rubs its back upon the window-panes*, a (restrictive) RC, also finite; and in (52), *that founded this organization* is (restrictive) RC which is finite.

B.

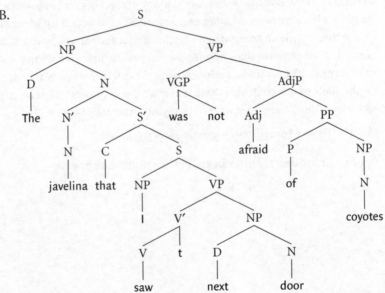

In (49), you could also argue that *exaggerated* is the past participle form of the verb and part of the VGP. Then, *is* will be an auxiliary, not a copula as in the tree below:

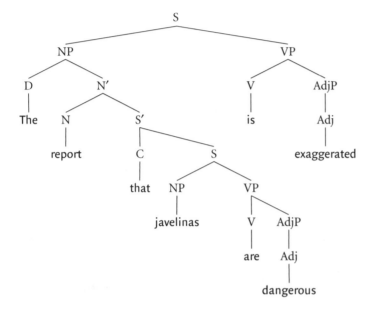

In (50), I have indicated that *soon* and *next door* are adverbials by making them sisters to V':

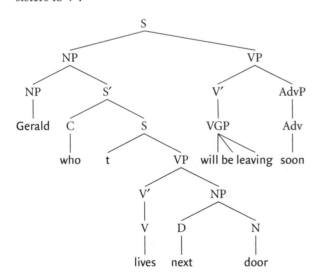

In (51), we just have an NP:

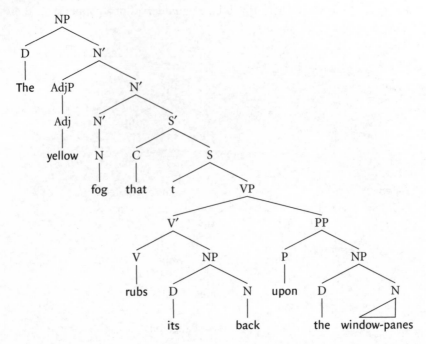

For (52):

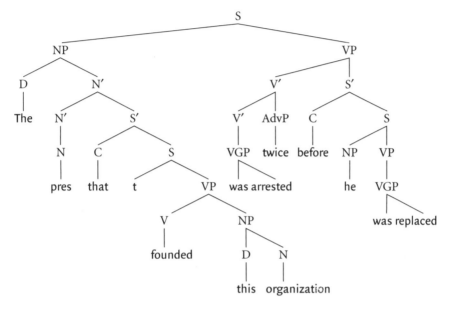

In (52), I have expressed that *twice* and *before he was replaced* are adverbials by making them sisters to V's. (Note that VGP is used when auxiliaries are present, but that V suffices when there is just the lexical verb).

C. To educate as the practice of freedom is a way of teaching [that anyone can learn]. That learning process comes easiest to those of us [who teach] [who also believe that there is an aspect of our vocation [that is sacred]]; [who believe that our work is not merely to share information but to share in the intellectual and spiritual growth of our students]. To teach in a manner [that respects and cares for the souls of our students] is essential if we are to provide the necessary conditions [where learning can most deeply and intimately begin].

D. The president that founded this organization was arrested twice before being replaced.

Special topic: who/m, which, that and preposition stranding

The rules are usually phrased as follows:

a. "The case of the pronouns *who* and *whom* depends on their function within their own clause. When a pronoun serves as the subject, use *who* or *whoever*;

when it functions as an object, use *whom* or *whomever*" (Holt, p. 376–7).

b.   "*who* refers to people of to animals that have names. *Which* and *that* usually refer to objects, events, or animals and sometimes to groups of people" (Holt, p. 381).

c.   Do not strand prepositions.

Fowler has definite ideas on all of these issues. In the older edition, he says: "Relative pronouns are as troublesome to the inexpert but conscientious writer as they are useful to everyone, which is saying much" (1926 [1950]: 709). Other style books have similar ideas.

The choice between nominative or accusative case has been talked about in the special topic to Chapter 4, as well as briefly in the chapter above. The only position where speakers still use *whom* is directly following a preposition, as in (54):

54.   This is a man about whom I know very little.

The debate on use of *who, which,* or *that* is a very lively one. Many argue that *that* can only be used in restrictive relatives when the antecedent is non-human. Sentence (55) violates both:

55.   Shakespeare, *King Lear* II, 4, 128
      ' was her Brother, that in pure kindnesse to his Horse, buttered his Hay.

Fowler is careful about criticizing the use of *that* and thinks it will change (1926[1950]: 716) "at present there is much more reluctance to apply *that* to a person than to a thing. Politeness plays a great part".

The dislike of stranding prepositions started allegedly with John Dryden. Many 'good' writers employ constructions as in (35) above with stranded prepositions, and would rewrite (54) as (56). Sir Winston Churchill is said to have ridiculed the construction by uttering (57):

56.   This is a man (who) I know little about.

57.   This is something up with which I will not put.

Stranding prepositions does not just occur with relatives, but with questions as well. An example of a stranded preposition in a question is (58):

58.   Who does he not want to put up with?

11 Special sentences

In this chapter, I discuss sentences in which elements have moved around for a particular reason, e.g. to ask a question, to make an exclamation, or to emphasize something (through topicalization, passive, cleft, and pseudo-cleft, to be explained below). Question sentences are referred to as interrogatives, whereas most of the sentences we have seen up to now assert something and are called indicatives. In Chapter 6, we briefly saw that sentences can also be used for commands, they then usually lack a subject, and are called imperatives. I won't come back to these here.

1. Questions/Interrogatives

Questions can be main clauses (*Will she leave?*) or embedded clauses (*I wonder if she'll leave*, see Chapter 7 for the latter kind). They can also be classified according to whether the entire sentence is questioned, in which case a Yes or No answer is expected, or whether another element is questioned using a *wh*-word (sometimes called an interrogative pronoun) such as *who, what, why,* etc., in which case a full answer is expected.

1.1 *Yes/No* questions

In *Yes/No* questions, the only appropriate answer is *Yes* or *No* (or *perhaps/ maybe*). To make a question, e.g. of (1), the auxiliary is fronted, as in (2):

1. She has gone.
2. Has she gone?

If there is no auxiliary present, as discussed in Chapter 6, a dummy *do* is used, as in (3):

3. Did you see Santa?

A structure for *Yes/No* Questions is given in (4), where the auxiliary moves to C (indicated by a trace):

4.

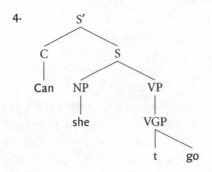

One piece of evidence for this movement to C is that when the complementizer is filled as in subordinate clauses such as (5), this movement is not possible:

5. *I wondered whether can she go.

1.2 *wh*-questions

The characteristics of a *wh*-clause that is a main clause are that it starts with a *wh*-word (*who, what, why, when, where, how*) and that the auxiliary is in second position. There is also an empty position in the sentence, indicated by a *t*. Examples are given in (6) to (8):

6. Who will you see t?
7. How heavy is that package t?
8. How much wood would a wood chuck chuck t, if a wood chuck could chuck wood?

Evidence for the presence of the trace is that, with special intonation, movement is not necessary. Thus, (9) is possible with emphasis on *what*:

9. You saw WHAT?

Questions such as (9) are called 'echo-questions'.

Some people have argued that the C position in (6) to (8) can contain both the *wh*-word and the auxiliary. Others have argued that there are two separate positions. Therefore, in this book, a structure for (6) to (8) will not be given.

2. Exclamations

Sentences such as (10) can be analyzed as in (4) above, namely as structures where the *what a nasty person* is in C. Notice that in sentences such as (10), the auxiliary does not move, unlike in (6):

10. What a nasty person he is t!

3. Topicalization, passive, cleft, and pseudo-cleft

Even though the structures of topicalizations, clefts, and passives look very different, they have in common that the order of words is rearranged, i.e. that they all involve movement. In English, old information is usually given in the beginning of the sentence, as in (11), and often preceded by *as for*, as in (12):

11. That book, I love.
12. and as for herself, she was too much provoked ...
    (Jane Austen, *Emma*, Vol 1, chap 15)

If the old information comes first, the readers or listeners can prepare themselves for the new information that comes later in the sentence. Thus, topicalizations as in (11) and (12) serve to front old information. The difference between (11) and (12) is that in (12) the topicalized element is repeated by means of a pronoun, whereas it is not in (11).

In the same way, passives and clefts can shift phrases to put old information at the beginning and new at the end. In a passive, as seen in Chapters 4 and 6, the subject *she* in (13) is the object *her* of the corresponding active in (14). This shifts the attention:

13. She was persuaded to go.
14. He persuaded her to go.

Examples of a cleft and pseudo-cleft are given in (15) and (16). A possible structure of clefts is that of a restrictive relative clause, as in (17) (note that I have represented an NP and PP by means of a 'coathanger' since the internal structure is not relevant here). The structure of pseudo-clefts is controversial and will not be given:

15. It was on the wedding-day of this beloved friend that Emma first sat in mournful thought of any continuance.
    (Jane Austen, *Emma*, vol 1, chap 1)

16.   What was irritating was that the disk collapsed.

17.

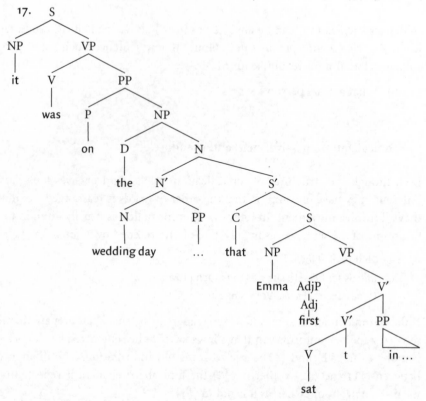

4.   Conclusion

In this chapter, I briefly describe a number of special constructions. Except for the *Yes/No* question and the cleft, tree structures are not provided. Key terms are **questions (WH and Yes/No); exclamations; topicalization, cleft, pseudo-cleft, and passive.**

Exercises

A. Identify the special constructions in:

   18. It is his character I despise.

   19. She was recognized going into the store.

   20. Higgins I hate.

   21. Who did Anne say that she saw?

B. Draw a tree for:

   22. Will she go then?

C. Explain the ambiguity in the following headline:

   23. Stolen Painting Found by Tree.

Keys to the Exercises

A. Sentence (18) is a cleft; (19) a passive; (20) a topicalization, and (21) a *wh*-question.

B.

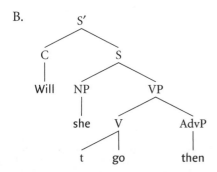

Notice that I have not been careful with the AdvP in B!

C. The sentence can be a passive in which case the meaning is strange/funny since typically trees are inanimate objects and don't find things. The intended meaning is not a passive, but one where *by tree* is a place adverbial and the finder has been left out or is unknown.

Special topic: Comma punctuation

Commas are used in writing to indicate a pause in speech. Pauses help disambiguate structural ambiguities, i.e. are syntactic in nature. In earlier English, e.g. in Chaucer and Shakespeare, punctuation is not used to express grammatical information. The discussion here is not meant to be exhaustive but merely discusses commas in connection to some of the constructions dealt with in this book. The main use of commas is to indicate that some information is not crucial. Since objects and complements are more important than modifiers and adverbials, we don't use commas for the former but we may do so for modifiers and adverbials (some people argue that one must use them there). Some specific rules:

a. Commas are not used inside the core sentence. Subjects, as in (24), cannot be separated from their verbs. Commas cannot appear around objects, or subject/object predicates. They are not used for complement clauses in an NP or AdjP, as in (25):

    24. *That he met Arafat, was untrue.
    25. *The story, that he met Arafat, is untrue.

b. Commas may be used for non-restrictive relative clauses, as in (26), and for adverbial clauses, as in (27). Sentence adverbials are typically surrounded by commas, as in (28) and (29):

    26. Pure Empiricism, which he was disposed not to accept, leads to scepticism.
    27. While he was gone, there were lots of parties at his house.
    28. Unfortunately, the sentence remained ungrammatical.
    29. The sentence, however, remains ungrammatical.

c. Commas are not used between independent clauses, as in (30). This construction is called comma splice:

    30. Scientists think they have detected life on the Moon, visions of people living in lunar colonies that stop off to refuel on the way to Mars can be envisaged.

I'll now give some examples where pauses in speech/commas in writing do make a difference. The well-known (31) is ambiguous, when pronounced without pauses or written without commas:

    31. Woman without her man is a savage.

The two possible sentences are either (32) or (33):

32. Woman, without her, man is a savage.
33. Woman, without her man, is a savage.

The tree structure of (33) is as in (34), with *woman* the subject and *is a savage* as the predicate. The structure of (32) is more complex since it is topicalized and, as shown in (35), *man* is the subject and *is a savage* is the predicate:

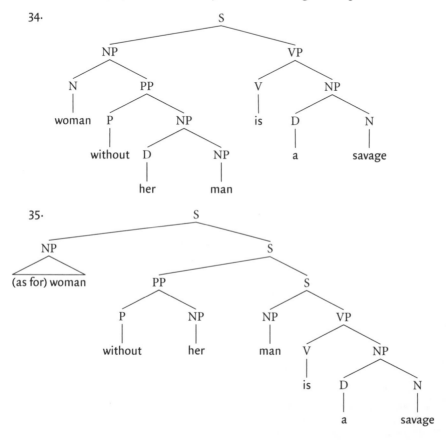

A construction where there is no agreement about when to use commas in coordinating three or more elements is (36). Some argue that all commas should be present in (36), e.g. Fowler and Oxford University Press; others argue the last can be left out. Allegedly, it once became the matter of a law suit, when something like (37) appeared in a will:

36. The books, magazines, and records in this store are on sale.
37. Equal parts of the estate will go to Mary, Jane, Edward and Michael.

188 An Introduction to the Grammar of English

Apparently, Mary and Jane assumed they would each get a third and Edward and Michael each a sixth, whereas Edward and Michael assumed each would get a quarter.

Review Chapters 9–11

In Chapters 9 and 10, the inner structure of the phrase is examined. PPs and AdvP are the simplest: PPs have a head and a complement and AdvPs have a modifier and a head. NPs and AdjPs are more complex. The NP can have a determiner, a head, several modifiers (both preceding and following the head) and a complement (either preceding or following the head); the AdjP can have a modifier preceding the head and a complement following the head. DON'T memorize this; just be able to analyze a given sentence. Chapter 11 gives examples of some special effect sentences such as topicalizations, passives, questions, and clefts. Again, just be prepared to recognize these.

Rather than providing separate exercises, I include a homework exercise that covers these chapters. No key is given for this. To help review what we have covered in the book as a whole, I include two final exams. Again, no keys are provided for these.

Homework, covering Chapters 7–11.

In the text below:

A. Locate the relative clauses and indicate whether they are restrictive or non-restrictive.

B. Find all the finite verbs and indicate whether or not they are lexical.

C. Analyze the last sentence of the first paragraph in terms of basic sentence structure. Try to draw a tree.

D. Draw a tree for the NP *its practitioners' insistence ... being considered* (second paragraph)

E. How might one analyse a sentence with *if* as in (last but one sentence in the second paragraph).

Text

From Kuhn "Mathematical versus Experimental Traditions in the Development of Physical Science"

Anyone who studies the history of scientific development repeatedly encounters a question, one version of which would be, "Are the sciences one or many?" Ordinarily that question is evoked by concrete problems of narrative organization, and these become especially acute when the historian of science is asked to survey his subject in lectures or in a book of significant scope. Should he take up the sciences one by one, beginning, for example, with mathematics, proceeding to astronomy, then to physics, to chemistry, to anatomy, physiology, botany, and so on? Or should he reject the notion that his object is a composite account of individual fields and take it instead to be knowledge of nature *tout court*? In that case, he is bound, insofar as possible, to consider all scientific subject matters together, to examine what men knew about nature at each period of time, and to trace the manner in which changes in method, in philosophical climate, or in society at large have affected the body of scientific knowledge conceived as one.

Given a more nuanced description, both approaches can be recognized as long-traditional and generally noncommunicating historiographic modes. [note deleted] The first, which treats science as at most a loose-linked congeries of separate sciences, is also characterized by its practitioners' insistence on examining closely the technical content, both experimental and theoretical, of past versions of the particular specialty being considered. That is a considerable merit, for the sciences are technical, and a history which neglects their content often deals with another enterprise entirely, sometimes fabricating it for the purpose. On the other hand, historians who have aimed to write the history of a technical specialty have ordinarily taken the bounds of their topic to be those prescribed by recent textbooks in the corresponding field. If, for example, their subject is electricity, then their definition of an electrical effect often closely resembles the one provided by modern physics. With it in hand, they may search ancient, medieval, and early modern sources for appropriate references, and an impressive record of gradually accumulating knowledge of nature sometimes results.

Examples of final exams

Example 1:

Please read the following text. Most questions are based on it. It is adapted from *The New York Times*, 4 December 1996.

The Moon May have Water

Scientists think they have detected water on the Moon. Suddenly, visions of people living in lunar colonies that stop off to refuel on the way to Mars are less far-fetched. After two years of careful analysis, scientists said yesterday that radar signals from an American spacecraft indicated the moon was not bone-dry. The spacecraft's radar signatures suggested the presence of water ice in the permanently cold shadows of a deep basin near the lunar south pole.

The survey revealed a vast landscape in which ice crystals are mixed with dirt. It seems a kind of permafrost that is presumably the residue of moisture from comets striking the Moon over the last three billion years.

Even though scientists are not positive, they see signals consistent with ice. Dr. Paul Spudis, one of the scientists reporting on the discovery, acknowledged that the discovery needed to be confirmed by an independent investigation. That might come a year from now because then another spacecraft will orbit the Moon with instruments of even greater precision for determining the presence of lunar water.

This discovery gives astronauts hope for longer stays in space. Told of the new discovery, Dr. Story Musgrave was very enthusiastic. He said that this implied there might be water and water is extraordinarily important to establishing a permanent base on the Moon. Other scientists reacted to the report with a mixture of caution and enthusiasm. They noted that the radar results were particularly difficult to interpret.

A. List all PPs used as adverbials in the first paragraph (or underline them clearly in the text).

B. Indicate function and name (or realization) of the phrases at sentence/ clause level in the sentences/clauses below, e.g. *the world is round*: SU: NP/Pred: VP/SubjPr: AdjP. **Do not analyse these units any further.**

  1. Suddenly, visions of people living in lunar colonies that stop off to refuel on the way to Mars are less far-fetched.

2. The survey revealed a vast landscape in which ice crystals are mixed with dirt.
3. ... another spacecraft will orbit the Moon with instruments of even greater precision for determining the presence of lunar water.
4. This discovery gives astronauts hope for longer stays in space.

C. Draw trees for the following phrases (use NP, N, D etc.):

1. The spacecraft's radar signatures
2. a kind of permafrost that is presumably the residue of moisture from comets striking the Moon over the last three billion years

D. Locate all non-finite clauses in the third paragraph. List them here or underline them clearly in the text.

E. What is the function and name of the following phrases in the structures in which they occur (e.g. Su/NP):

1. positive (l. 10)
2. consistent with ice (l. 10)
3. Told of the new discovery (ll. 16–7)
4. that the radar results were particularly difficult to interpret (ll. 18–9)

F. List the postmodifiers in the fourth paragraph. Also indicate what their name is (e.g. PP, Restrictive or Non-Restrictive Relative Clause, etc.)

G. List all auxiliaries. Indicate what kind they are (perfect ...)

H. Draw trees for:

1. After two years of careful analysis, scientists said yesterday that radar signals from an American spacecraft indicated the moon was not bone-dry.
2. Dr. Paul Spudis, one of the scientists reporting on the discovery, acknowledged that the discovery needed to be confirmed by an independent investigation.
3. He said that this implied there might be water and water is extraordinarily important to establishing a permanent base on the Moon.

Example 2:

A Life of Fiction
adapted from Jane Smiley
(NYT Magazine, 3/12/2000)

When Charles Dickens was traveling home from France in June 1865, the train he was riding in went off the tracks while crossing a bridge over a river. Seven first-class carriages dropped into the river. The eighth, which was the one Dickens was travelling in, dangled off the bridge. Dickens calmed his companions and clambered out. He was indefatigable and helped to free his friends in the carriage and many others.

When all that could be done for the victims had been done, Dickens, who was 53 years old and not in very good health, climbed into the carriage again and retrieved from the pocket of his coat the installment of 'Our Mutual friend' he had just finished.

The author, who hadn't shrunk from describing the lurid and the terrible before, made no effort to describe what he had seen. "I don't know what to call the accident" he wrote to a friend. He also refused to give testimony to the subsequent inquest. Why did Dickens hide his heroism? It so happens that Dickens' traveling companions were his mistress Ellen Ternan and her mother. What is really interesting is that a man whose volume of writings approach logorrhea could dissemble his most intimate concerns and feelings so consistently and for so long.

A. Please list all adverbials in the second paragraph.

B. Please list all PPs that function as modifiers in the first paragraph.

C. Indicate function and name of the phrases/clauses at sentence level, e.g. Su/NP; Adverbial/PP in the sentences below. Do not go further than the first layer:

    a. I don't know what to call the accident

    b. When all that could be done for the victims had been done, Dickens, who was 53 years old and not in very good health, climbed into the carriage again

    c. ... helped to free his friends in the carriage and many others

D. What is the function and name of the following:

    a. his mistress ... mother (l. 15)

    b. testimony (l. 13)

      c. off the bridge (l. 4)

      d. a man ... logorrhea (ll. 16–7)

E. List all auxiliaries in the second paragraph. Indicate what kind they are.

F. List all finite verbs in the third paragraph.

G. Indicate the relative clauses in the first and second paragraphs. Are they restrictive or non-restrictive?

H. Draw trees for:

      a. The author, who hadn't shrunk from describing the lurid and the terrible before, made no effort to describe what he had seen.

      b. I found Friday's lecture very stimulating.

Further reading

This section provides some references to more detailed discussions of the material covered in each of the chapters. I have tried to keep it brief. In general, Quirk et al. (1985) is a very good source for getting more information on grammatical constructions, e.g. what kinds of adverbs there are. It is not good on getting a general picture (close to 1800 pages), but is very comprehensive.

Crystal (1987) is an excellent (and nicely presented) introduction to linguistic topics such as writing systems, phonetics, dictionaries, names, languages in the world, language acquisition, and sign language. Other introductions are Fromkin & Rodman (1998) and O'Grady et al. (1993).

There are several websites (with listservs) that may be interesting. For general linguistics, there is the linguist list at http://www.emich.edu/~linguist. They have a list of all language related lists and serve as archive. You might also check the links at www.public.asu.edu/~gelderen/links.htm. For the History of English, there is a site at: http://ebbs.english.vt.edu/hel/hel.html and for the American Dialect Society, there is a site at: http://www.americandialect.org. There are a number of sites devoted to how grammar improves writing, e.g. at www.phon.ucl.ac.uk/home/dick/writing.htm, or see Hudson (1992).

Further reading to Chapter 1

For more information on sociolinguistics, see e.g. Wardhaugh (1992); for more on prescriptivism, see e.g. Finegan (1980); Quinn (1980); Crystal (1987, Chapter 1). Fowler (1926 [1950], and also http://www.bartleby.com/116/) contains many prescriptive rules, and so does Strunk (see e.g. http://www.bartleby.com/141/).

Additional information on Universal Grammar and innate ideas can be found in Chomsky (1975; 1995). Newmeyer (1998) provides some background on the different linguistic schools. For more on language change, see Aitchison

(1985), and on the use of 'right words', see Wells (1973); Baugh & Cable (1993, Chapters 8 and 9). If you'd like to know more on Linguistics in general, see Crystal (1987), Brinton (2000), and O'Grady et al. (1987). For more instances of humor in language, see Nilsen & Nilsen (2000).

To Chapter 2

For more on the distinction between adjectives and adverbs, see Swan (1980); on prepositions, see Quirk et al. (1985:661 ff.); on coordinators and complementizers, see Quirk et al. (1985: Chapters 13 and 14); on categories in general, see Radford (1988:56–64; 1997:37–58). For differences in categories among languages, see van Gelderen (1993), and on the use of grammatical categories in creoles and 'proto-language', see Bickerton (1990). On the view that grammatical categories also head phrases, see Chomsky (1986). This is now the accepted position in syntax but is not followed in this book since it would be too different from traditional grammatical structures.

To Chapter 3

On phrases, Radford (1988, chap 2–3) might be helpful; for a very detailed work on coordination in a variety of languages, see Johannessen (1998). On Multiple Negation, see Jespersen (1940: Chapter 23), and Labov (1972).

To Chapter 4

For more on functions, consult Quirk et al. (1985: Chapter 16). On the different kinds of indirect objects, see Herriman (1995). Curme (1931:27) provides a list of 60 or so copulas. Information on Old English case can be found in Quirk & Wrenn (1957).

To Chapter 5

On prepositional, phrasal, and phrasal prepositional verbs, see Quirk et al. (1985:1150–1157; 1178–9); on phrasal verbs, see Radford (1988:89–101).

Cowie & Mackin's (1975) dictionary is helpful for combinations of Vs and Ps that are unknown to English speakers. See Levin (1994) for very careful distinctions of the different verbs. On the earliest use of the split infinitive, see van Gelderen (1993).

To Chapter 6

For more on auxiliaries in general, see McCawley (1988, chap 8); Quirk et al. (1985: 120–171); for more on a non-flat structure see van Gelderen (1997b); for more on finiteness, see Quirk et al. (1985: 96–7).

To Chapter 7

About *like*, see Underhill (1988); Ferrara & Bell (1995); Tagliamonte & Hudson (1999); Macaulay (2001). To read how the S′ is replaced by CP, see e.g. Chomsky (1986: 2–4), van Gelderen (1993: chap 1); note that this is somewhat difficult reading.

To Chapter 8

For more on non-finite clause, see Quirk et al. (1985: Chapter 14); on dangling modifiers, see Quinn (1980: 112–4); and Strunk at www.bartleby/141/strunk.html#7.

To Chapter 9

For more on the structure of the NP, see Quirk et al. (1985: chap. 17), and also Burton-Roberts (1977: chap 7), but note that by the latter NOM is used for N′. For more on the distinction between complements and modifiers, see Hornstein & Lightfoot (1981: Introduction) and Radford (1988: chap 3).

Information on Old English agreement can be found in Quirk & Wrenn (1957), and on 'mistakes' with agreement, see van Gelderen (1997a).

To Chapter 10

On clausal complements to adjectives, see Quirk et al. (1985:1220 ff.) and to nouns, see Quirk et al. (1985:1244–1274). For more on the structure of relative clauses, see Radford (1988:480–492).

Further reading for Chapter 11

For use of the CP to account for questions, please see Radford (1997: chap 7). On special constructions, see Quirk et al. (1985: Chapter 18); for a prescriptivist view on avoiding the passive, see Strunk at www.bartleby.com/141/strunk#11. Information on drawing trees for *wh*-questions can be found in Radford (1997: chap 7). On punctuation, see a writing guide, such as *The Holt Handbook*; or Strunk at www.bartleby.com/141.

References

Aitchison, Jean. 1985. *Language Change: Progress or Decay?* New York: Universe Books.

Barry, Anita. 1998. *English Grammar: Language as human behavior.* Upper Saddle River, NJ. Prentice Hall.

Baugh, Albert & Thomas Cable 1993. *A History of the English Language.* Fourth edition. London: RKP.

Bickerton, Derek 1990. *Language and Species.* Chicago: University of Chicago Press.

Brinton, Laurel 2000. *The Structure of Modern English.* Amsterdam/Philadelphia: John Benjamins.

Burton-Roberts, N. 1977. *Analysing Sentences.* London: Longman.

Chomsky, N. 1975. *Reflections on Language.* New York: Pantheon.

——— 1986. *Barriers.* Cambridge: MIT Press.

——— 1995. *The Minimalist Program.* Cambridge: MIT Press.

Cowie, A. & R. Mackin 1975. *Oxford Dictionary of Current Idiomatic English.* London: Oxford University Press.

Crystal, David 1987. *The Cambridge Encyclopedia of Language.* Cambridge University Press.

Curme, George 1931. *A grammar of the English Language* vol 2. D.C. Heath & Company.

Ferrara, Kathleen & Barbara Bell 1995. "Sociolinguistic Variation and Discourse function of constructed dialogue introducers: the case of *be + like*". *American Speech* 70.3.

Finegan, Edward 1980. *Attitudes toward English Usage.* New York: Teachers College Press.

Fowler, H. W. 1926 [1950]. *A Dictionary of Modern English Usage.* Oxford: Clarendon.

Fromkin, Victoria & Robert Rodman 1998. *An Introduction to Language.* Sixth edition. Harcourt Brace.

Gelderen, Elly van 1993. *The Rise of Functional Categories.* Amsterdam: Benjamins.

——— 1997a. *Verbal Agreement and the Grammar behind its 'Breakdown': Minimalist Feature Checking.* Tübingen: Niemeyer.

——— 1997b. "Structures of Tense and Aspect", *Linguistic Analysis* 27.3–4: 138–165.

Henry, Alison 1995. *Belfast English and Standard English: Dialect Variation and Parameter Setting.* Oxford: Oxford University Press.

Herriman, Jennifer 1995. *The Indirect Object in Present Day English.* Göteborg: Acta Universitatis.

Hornstein, Norbert & David Lightfoot (eds.) 1981. *Explanation in Linguistics.* London: Longman.

Hudson, Richard 1992. *Teaching Grammar: A Guide for the National Curriculum.* Oxford: Blackwell.

Jespersen, Otto. 1940. *A Modern English Grammar V*. London: Allen & Unwin [reprint].

Johannessen, Janne Bondi 1998. *Coordination*. Oxford: Oxford University Press.

Kirszner, Laurie & Stephen Mandell 1992. *The Holt Handbook*. Third edition. Fort Worth, TX: Harcourt Brace Javanovich.

Labov, William 1972. "Negative Attraction and Negative Concord", in *Language in the Inner City*. Philadelphia: University of Pennsylvania Press.

Levin, Beth 1994. *English Verb Classes and Alterations*. Chicago: University of Chicago Press.

Macaulay, Ronald 2001. "*You're like 'why not'*: the quotative expressions of Glasgow adolescents". *Journal of Sociolinguistics* 5.1: 3–21.

McCawley, James 1988. *The Syntactic Phenomena of English* Vol 1 and 2. Chicago: University of Chicago Press.

Newmeyer, Frederick 1998. *Language Form and Language Function*. Cambridge: MIT Press.

Nilsen, Alleen & Don Nilsen 2000. *Encyclopedia of 20th-Century American Humor*. Phoenix: The Oryx Press.

Oxford English Dictionary (OED). 2nd edition on CD Rom. Oxford: Oxford University Press.

O'Dwyer, Bernard 2000. *Modern English Structures*. Broadview Press.

O'Grady, William & Michael Dobrovolsky 1987. *Contemporary Linguistic Analysis*. First edition. Toronto: Copp, Clark Pitman.

Quinn, Jim. 1980. *American Tongue and Cheek*. Harmondsworth: Penguin Books.

Quirk, Randolph & Sidney Greenbaum 1973. *A University Grammar of English*. London: Longman.

Quirk, Randolph, Sidney Greenbaum, Geoffrey Leech, & Jan Svartvik 1985. *A Comprehensive Grammar of the English Language*. London: Longman.

Quirk, Randolph & C. Wrenn 1957. *An Old English Grammar*. Second edition. London: Methuen.

Radford, Andrew 1988. *Transformational Grammar*. Cambridge: Cambridge University Press.

——— 1997. *Syntactic Theory and the Structure of English*. Cambridge: Cambridge University Press.

Strunk, William with E.B. White 1959[2000]. *The Elements of Style*. Boston: Allyn and Bacon.

Swan, Michael 1980. *Practical English Usage*. Oxford: Oxford University Press.

Tagliamonte, Sali & Rachel Hudson 1999. "*Be like* et al. beyond America: The quotative system in British and Canadian youth". *Journal of Sociolinguistics* 3.2: 147–172.

Underhill, Robert 1988. "*Like* is, like, focus", *American Speech* 63.3: 234–246.

Verspoor, Marjolijn & Kim Sauter 2000. *English Sentence Analysis*. Amsterdam/Philadelphia: John Benjamins.

Wardhaugh, Ronald 1992. *An Introduction to Sociolinguistics*. Second edition. Oxford: Blackwell.

Wells, Ronald. 1973. *Dictionaries and the Authoritarian Tradition*. Den Haag: Mouton.